PILGRIMS' TALES ... AND MORE

Edited by Mary McDaid and Pat McHugh

Pilgrims' Tales
... and More

the columba press

First published in 2000 by
the columba press
55A Spruce Avenue, Stillorgan Industrial Park,
Blackrock, Co Dublin

Cover by Bill Bolger
Origination by The Columba Press
Printed in Ireland by Colour Books Ltd, Dublin

ISBN 1 85607 297 5

Contents

Preface

For at least one thousand years, and probably many more, the story and stories of Lough Derg have been told. That unique place belongs to those who go there as pilgrims. This collection of reflections and stories seeks to honour that ownership. The place and the experience are such that only a morsel of its narrative can ever be told. The entire discourse is known only to God. The reader will find in these pages, however, a series of insights and sacred moments from the pens and camera of the contributors which offer glimpses of a reality well beyond the known face of Lough Derg. Included are two pieces which were written over a hundred years ago and never previously published. They were found in Clogher's diocesan archives.

A constant feature of Lough Derg's ongoing story is the widely representative group of people who come on pilgrimage; this remains true whether the pilgrims are counted in tens, hundreds or thousands. The invitation to contribute to this gathering of memories and impressions sought to reflect that wide representation. Thanks to all those who responded; in doing so they entrust their story to all who read it; may it be deeply respected.

The compilation and editing of this work has given us a deepened appreciation of Lough Derg, the place and the experience; may it be so for the reader as well.

Anonymous

Biking to Purgatory
(Written circa 1898)

Do not imagine from the above title that I am about giving you any mystic account of adventures on a bicycle to that place where some of us hope not to have to spend too long. I am merely going to recount how I travelled on a bicycle across Ireland from Belfast to St Patrick's Purgatory on Station Island in Lough Dearg, County Donegal. Many generations of my ancestors travelled to Lough Dearg on foot from their Ulster homes, while my parents and I always went there by steamer and railway, but I was the first of our people who went by the present popular method of transit.

The first thought that suggested itself to me when the bicycle came completely under my control was how soon would practice at it enable me to bring it with me to Ireland and make the pilgrimage to Lough Dearg on the *capall iarann* (iron horse). So, as summer came round, I made the necessary preparations to occupy most of my short vacation wheeling across Ireland.

Arrived at Belfast and put up at the Linen Hall Hotel, I took up the G. N. Railway's (Ireland) timetable and from it I learned that the nearest railway station to Lough Dearg was 190¾ miles from Belfast which, of course, was too much for me to do in one day, especially as I had ample time and wished to see all I could along the way. Let me here parenthetically warn those who follow me that there will appear some confusion and a considerable amount of contradiction as to distances. This arises from the fact that the railways are measured in statute miles and the roads are measured in Irish miles. The statute mile, or, as it is called in Ireland, the English mile, is about eleven-fourteenths of the Irish mile. The police and the cyclists will give the distance in

English miles while most of the country people will give it in Irish miles.

Starting early from Belfast on Tuesday morning and going west, I passed through Lisburn, Lurgan, Portadown, and at Armagh I stopped to refresh myself at the Charlemount Arms Hotel and took a short run round to see the Catholic and Protestant Cathedrals and started for Monaghan which I reached late in the evening, after having travelled over 43 Irish miles (54 statute). I put up for the night at Miss Curran's Temperance Hotel and paid a visit to the grand Catholic Cathedral of St Macartan. Another early start – I left Monaghan in a south-westerly direction by the Clones Road but soon turned to the west, leaving the main road and the railway behind me, and made for Rosslea and did not see the railway again until I came near Lisnaskea. This diversion, though at first it brought me over a hilly road for a couple of miles, still took several miles off my journey which I continued through Lisnaskea and, avoiding the railway and Maguiresbridge, passed Lisbellaw into Enniskillen.

At Enniskillen I refreshed myself in the Royal Hotel and started along a splendid road between the railway and Lough Erne, through Lisnarrick and Kesh to Pettigo. This was the third time I took a 'short cut' of the railway and saved some miles by so doing. After a pleasant ride through a beautiful country, I reached Pettigo. I had been under the impression I was the first pilgrim who had come on a bike but found others had been before me and that Messrs Flood had a room at their hotel made ready for the reception of all sorts of cycles. Having seen my bike safely locked in this important room, I joined some other pilgrims in eating a good dinner at Flood's, not requiring the advice of one of my fellow-pilgrims to eat plenty then, for if I didn't I'd surely rue it to-morrow. Dinner over, two car loads of us left Flood's and a brisk drive of two miles brought us through an agricultural country into the mountains and ultimately to Lough Dearg's shore and before our gaze gradually unfolded its great sheet of water dotted with islands and surrounded by mountains.

It is many years since I first beheld the holy island and, although I have often visited it since, the same thrill and awe-inspiring feeling crept over me on this July morning in 1898 as did on the same spot eighteen years ago. As I stood near the ferry-house and looked towards Station Island – over a mile off – watching the pilgrims move about the island performing their 'stations' in the twilight, the same strange sensation crept over me that others and I have again and again felt at this spot. The sound of a horn on the island announcing the departure of a boat roused me from contemplating my feelings and in due course the boat reached us, discharging nine or ten pilgrims who had finished their station. I paid one of the Messrs Flood 9d for my car fare and 8d for my ticket for passage by the boat into which a dozen pilgrims entered – eight of us who came from Pettigo on cars and the remainder who came on foot over the mountains which surround the lake on every side. A quiet row across by exceedingly careful boatmen left us beside St Michael's Quay on the shore of Station Island. To the right of the passage or roadway leading from this little quay is St Mary's Church, neatly constructed, but very empty and bare-looking. On the left of the passage is a two-storied house, occupied by the clergy doing duty on the island and which is called the Prior's. Further on, adjoining the priest's house, is a row of lodging-houses, four in number. Then follows on the same side the hospice, the near end for males and the further end for females, and at the end of the hospice facing the quay but extending almost across the island which is narrower at that part is St Patrick's Church. It is older and not so neat as St Mary's Church. Immediately in front of the hospice, on three pedestals at short intervals, are three beautiful life-size marble statues of Our Blessed Lady, St Joseph, and St Patrick. The last is quite worthy of the patron of the island and is really a magnificent work of art. The space which lies between the churches and in front of the hospice is occupied by a rocky little hill on the top of which is the campanile, and among the rocks sloping towards St Patrick's Church are six stone circles, called beds, with a crucifix in the

centre of each. On my arrival I entered the hospice, and was
shown by the servant to a little room on a corridor consisting of
six similar rooms. Here I deposited my cycle-bag and went to
bed, where I slept soundly until awakened by the Angelus at 5
am. I dressed, substituted an old pair of trousers for my knickers, and bareheaded and barefooted proceeded into the open air
exactly as every other man on the island was attired. Before
going out I invested at 'the stall' in a sheet of paper containing
the directions as to prayers, etc., for which I paid one half-
penny. I found I had forgotten my Rosary beads and bought a
pair at 'the stall', which one of the priests whom I met in the hospice blessed. Thus fully equipped, I set out on my station.

On going out of the hospice I could not resist the uncontrol-
lable desire of standing near St Joseph's statue and gazing on a
sight I had often looked at before. A continuous stream of men
and women, all the former and some of the latter bareheaded,
but all barefooted, passed slowly and silently round the stone
circles; their lips were moving in silent prayer, and when they
passed near me I could hear the whispered Pater, Ave, or Creed.
They seemed like souls passing from this earth into the here-
after, and were at once suggestive of the thoughts of what will
follow immediately after our deathbeds. At this point I was
roused from my reverie by some Belfast friends, who informed
me they had come by train the evening before, and were in bed
when I arrived. We all went into St Patrick's Church and heard
early Mass and a short discourse from the Prior. Some of my
friends had never been here before and were loud in their praises
of the pilgrimage, as is everybody else who has gone through it.

After a short conversation with my friends, we began our
first 'station' by entering St Patrick's Church and paying a short
visit to the Blessed Sacrament. We thence proceeded out of the
church to St Patrick's Cross, kneeling at the foot of which we
said a Pater, and Ave, and a Creed. This cross consisted of a
round stone pillar, with a small metal cross fastened into the top
of it. The pillar is a remnant of ancient times, which escaped
complete destruction by the English Protestant soldiers and sur-

vived for centuries. I say complete, for it has been broken near the pedestal, and the side of the socket at the top is smashed, showing the violence with which the original crucifix was torn or probably hammered away. Other pilgrims who began the station along with me formed a little group around St Patrick's Cross, and when we had finished the above-mentioned prayers, we proceeded around St Patrick's Church, until we came to St Brigid's Cross, a cross cut in a slab in a corner of St Patrick's Church ; here we again knelt and recited three Paters, three Aves and one Creed. These finished, we each stood in turn with our backs to the cross, stretched out our arms, and in the same silent whisper as we prayed, renounced three times the world, the flesh, and the devil. This done, we walked seven times round St Patrick's Church, each time reciting a decade of the Rosary, and during the last circuit we added the Creed. Thence we proceeded to St Brigid's Bed, around the outside of which we walked three times, saying the three Paters, three Aves and a Creed. We repeated the same prayers kneeling at the entrance, while we made three internal circuits, and while we knelt at the foot of the crucifix in the centre. The same prayers and exercises were gone through by us in succession at St Brendan's Bed, St Catherine's Bed, and St Colmcille's Bed. There are two other stone circles which touch each other, of different sizes, the smaller dedicated to St Molaise, and the larger to St Patrick. Here is the first encroachment on olden times I must notice, for when I went there first the pilgrims used to make nine circuits of these two beds, reciting nine Paters, nine Aves and one Creed. We were now only required by the programme to make six circuits, repeating six Paters, six Aves and one Creed. I may remark that although we were required to say three Paters, three Aves, and a Creed, during the circuits of the other beds, and double the number at these, I was always able to get over more Paters and Aves than the requisite number, for most of us can pray faster than we can walk – at least at Lough Dearg. Kneeling at the entrance to each of these, and during the internal circuits, and kneeling at the crucifixes in the centre of each, we recited the three Paters, three

Aves and one Creed. I noticed most people mistook St Molaise's Bed for St Patrick's, and ended their rounds of the beds at it instead of St Patrick's. This being a mere altering of course is of no consequence. Having finished the beds we proceeded to the eastern side of the Island, and standing at the water's edge (almost all the pilgrims stood in the water), we recited five Paters, five Aves and a Creed. We then came in and knelt on the shore, where we repeated the same prayers. Leaving the shore we returned to St Patrick's Cross, where one Pater, Ave and Creed were said kneeling. We then entered St Patrick's Church, where we formed a little group, and said five decades of the Rosary together. Thus ended our first station and we went out to have a chat. We all felt well and those who had never been there before seemed in high spirits at discovering they were so well able to perform the station. I had two more stations to do to complete the day's work.

After refreshing myself with a cup of 'wine', i.e. a cup of boiled water sweetened with sugar, I proceeded to make a second station in exactly the same manner, each station taking about one hour and ten minutes to accomplish.

As soon as I had completed my second station and taken another cup of wine, I retired to my bedroom in the hospice, where I read Chap. 53, Book III, and Chaps. 20 and 21 of Book I of the *Imitation*. This I followed with preparing for confession. This brought me close up to 4 pm when I thought it time to take my meal, and although I had been without food from the previous night, I never felt the pangs of hunger. Seated on a form in the refectory, a number of fellow-pilgrims and I partook of our meal, consisting of dry bread and black tea, over which we had a most interesting conversation and quite forgot the unpleasantness of our food. In addition to the plain white bread most of us indulged in oaten bread, which has always been the proper food of the pilgrimage. It is excellent fasting fare. A patriotic young man at the table assured us that it was on oaten bread the Irish soldiers subsisted during the wars with the English, which induced the 'lying English historians' who could not account for the endurance of the Irish 'creight', to invent the absurd myth that the Irish lived on shamrocks. Shortly after the meal I finished my third station, and as the Angelus was ringing while I was finishing, I entered St Patrick's Church with all the other pilgrims, and attended the evening devotions, during which we heard a most impressive sermon from a young priest attached to the island; that was followed by Benediction of the Blessed Sacrament. The choir, which was collected from amongst the congregation, though at times a little discordant, got on remarkably well. During the following couple of hours I again retired to my room and completed my preparation for confession and read a little more of the *Imitation*, and at nine o'clock the bell summoned us to St Patrick's Church, where the devotion of the Stations of the Cross was gone through, accompanied by the *Stabat Mater* from the choir.

When the ceremony had concluded, we went into the hospice, where I borrowed a topcoat from a new friend who had been up the night before, my friend stipulating that I should throw sand at his window the following morning. This was the first inconvenience I found through going on the bike. I could not carry a sufficiently heavy overcoat. All who were to sit up for the night took cups of 'wine' and we entered prison, i.e went into St Patrick's Chapel, for the night. The hours up to midnight were spent by different members of the congregation reading meditations aloud, alternated by others singing hymns. At midnight the man whose duty it was, announced that the stations were about to begin, and the entire congregation gathered close around the altar, and recited aloud the prayers we had said at the stations during the day, kneeling, standing, and moving about inside the church just as we had done around the beds in the daytime. The beginning and end of each portion was announced alternately by the man in charge and by a blind man called Dan. At the end of the first station most of the men who were there went out into the air to rouse themselves, and some of them to smoke. I moved some distance from the church and listened to the ripple of the waters on the shore and the rustle of the leaves on the only tree on the Island. I fell to thinking of many former events of my life, and on looking up to the heavens I beheld the wondrous firmament. I then thought of the immensity of space and of the power of the great Creator who made all those mighty constellations; anon of the infinitesimal part of creation I was, which of course led me to think on the mysteries and mercies of our redemption. From my reverie I was roused by the tinkle of the altar bells which announced the beginning of the second station. I hurried back to the church and went through the second station as I had done the first. Towards the end of this we all felt very sleepy. Many of those in 'prison' had snuff or head salts to assist in keeping them and their friends awake. I did not move so far from the church during the interval between the second and third stations but remained near the door conversing with the men about me for the fifteen minutes allowed.

The third station was performed like the previous one, with the difference that it was much harder to avoid falling asleep. When the concluding prayers had finished, the day had fully dawned and the bright morning promised a fine day. Soon after we got out, and after I had roused my friend by throwing sand at his window, the hospice was opened, and some sat down before the fire, while others, including myself, went to our rooms and had a wash and shave, and came down considerably roused and refreshed to Mass at five o'clock. It was with considerable difficulty I kept awake during Mass. My next neighbour had to nudge me several times to keep me from sleeping. After Mass all who had been in 'prison' the previous night attended at St Mary's Church where our names were entered in a book by the Prior. We paid the fees of the pilgrimage, 10d, and got a ticket for confession. During the couple of hours which intervened before the hearing of the confessions, most of us kept moving about watching other pilgrims going round the beds. Those who were not fortunate enough to prepare for confession the previous day, as I had done, had great difficulty in doing so, owing to the inroads sleep was making on them. My confession was over shortly before noon, and after being refreshed with a cup of 'wine' I made an extra station for deceased and absent friends, and a little after two o'clock I joined a pleasure party who went in a boat to Saints' Island where the Augustinian Monastery flourished in the Middle Ages but which was wrecked by English Protestant soldiers who left not a stone upon a stone of it.

Our row back and forwards was made pleasant by the singing of hymns and patriotic songs. We had one song in Irish. After our return we partook of dinner which was enjoyed just as much as any of us ever enjoyed a much more sumptuous repast. Some, like myself, took the 'wine' in preference to black tea, and oaten bread in preference to white bread. We chatted pleasantly over our meal. All were in good humour and in fact quite buoyant. As soon as we had finished I made another extra station for absent and dead friends which brought me up to the evening Angelus when we again repaired to St Patrick's Church for evening devotions. When I entered, the sleepiness had all gone from me, but returned during the sermon; however, after Benediction I felt no inclination to go to bed until after the Stations of the Cross at 9 pm. Along with many others in the hospice I washed my feet and hurried up to my room where I slept such a sleep as I had not enjoyed since my last visit to Lough Dearg. The morning bell brought myself and friends down to Mass and Holy Communion. The rest of the third day was spent in performing our three remaining stations and reading at intervals the *Imitation of Christ*, Chaps. 22, 23, and 24 of Book I, and Chaps. 14, 48, and 59 of Book III. We fasted and attended the devotion as on the previous days. Many went away fasting during the day. I thought it better to remain, so I ended my pilgrimage on the island by bathing my feet and going to bed.

I was sorry to observe some encroachments creeping in, e.g., some persons went to bed the morning after they got out of 'prison'. The old rule was that from 6 pm on the evening of the first day until bedtime on the second night you should not wilfully go to sleep. Other persons brought lemons with them and squeezed the juice into the 'wine'. This changed the nature of the drink, and, of course, is a departure from the ancient rule. I hope

the clergy will resist these inroads of modern luxury; for once
Lough Dearg loses its ancient customs it will be on the rapid
road to oblivion, for its very existence depends on a rigid adher-
ence to its time-honoured discipline which stamps it as the sole
survivor of the primitive faith of West Europe.

Amongst the pilgrims were people from all parts of Ireland
and several Irishmen and Irishwomen from England, Scotland,
and America, and what pride I felt at meeting men and women
of my Celtic race from so many lands, the brotherhood of which
Lough Dearg is the common tie, binding us scattered children of
the Gael and bidding us return again and again to this beatified
spot amid the homes of our sires.

On the next morning I resumed my knickers and stockings
and after some difficulty my boots, for my feet were swollen and
I had to bathe them in warm water before I could get the boots
on. After Mass and a very hearty breakfast with no trace of fasting fare in it, I paid the smallest hotel bill I have ever paid outside Lough Dearg and I started by an early boat, feeling quite
lonely at leaving the island. The extraordinary sensation of lone-
someness creeps over every one when leaving and I have experienced it each year since my first departure from St Michael's
Quay. When mounted on my bicycle, I rode straight back to the
Belfast steamer, though at a slower pace, owing to a little stiff-
ness caused by the penitential exercises of Lough Dearg.

Let me now advise every one of my readers who can spare
time to make a similar pilgrimage. Go between 1st and 30th July
(avoiding travelling on the 12th). The weather is pleasanter then.
If you go before the 1st there are seldom many persons on it, and
too few fellow-pilgrims make you feel not so comfortable, and if
you wait until August there will be too much of a crowd, which
is rather disagreeable, and you wont get a whole room to yourself. What strikes strangers most is the number of young men
amongst the pilgrims. It is quite edifying to see them frequently
exceed the number of women who go there. Every class and degree of Irish Catholics are met with there. Centuries upon centuries have looked down upon generation after generation of our

race going over the penances we go over now, and I pray God and St Patrick to preserve our old land and continue Lough Dearg a holy meeting-place for 'the sea-divided Gael'.

Willie Walsh

Contradiction and Challenge

I went back to Lough Derg in August 1999 after a gap of some thirty-five years. Yes, it is still tough going! It is still St Patrick's Purgatory. But then, of course, prayer, penance, fasting and vigils are at the heart of Christ's life and teaching.

The Lough Derg pilgrimage is something of a 'sign of contradiction' to today's Ireland where unit cost, competitiveness and profitability are the success words. Bare feet and empty stomachs are a nonsense in that world. And yet we need to remind ourselves that we live in a world where there are far too many bare feet and empty stomachs.

The Lough Derg pilgrimage is a challenge. It is a personal challenge to the individual about his/her own value system. It is a challenge to our modern society about the values by which it operates.

I believe that it is important that Lough Derg continue that challenge in the new century.

I'm glad I went back. And shoes and beds and food are all the more enjoyable after it!

Mary Wall

The converted sceptic

There is a long-standing myth that if you look back at the island from the boat as you leave Lough Derg, something about this strange and mystic place will keep drawing you back. Being gloriously unaware of the significance of this legend I have wondered on many an occasion why I keep returning!

Few words can be added to what has already been written and said about Lough Derg and each year as June arrives, dormitories, dry toast and oat biscuits are busily prepared in readiness for the influx of brave pilgrims who push themselves to the very limits of human endurance. For the 'regular' visitor to Lough Derg has the advantage (or is it disadvantage?) of knowing in advance what fate has in store.

I remember with great clarity my maiden voyage to St Patrick's Purgatory, which I freely confess was never done out of a great sense of religious conviction, but more out of curiosity. My mother, on the other hand, a deeply religious woman, had undertaken the said pilgrimage on many occasions and to her, and those of her generation, it was the ultimate declaration of Christian penance. It was also a pretty 'safe bet' that the eternal soul would be guaranteed easy passage when the time came. While a self-confessed sceptic, I somehow thought I should do it once, just to be on the safe side.

Without utterance to friend or foe and, more especially, as a cowardly excuse to avoid cynical comments from pagan, agnostic and atheist friends, I decided my venture should be undertaken with the minimum of fanfare and, initially, the outlook didn't seem all that bad. All was well with the world as I sat in blissful ignorance on a comfortable coach as it drove the beautiful winding roads of Donegal. Unspoilt roads that beheld the most magnificent hedgerows of wild scented pink flowers.

As we neared our destination the singing and light-hearted banter that had been part of the long trip suddenly came to an abrupt halt as the bus reached journey's end and everyone psyched themselves up in readiness. Catching the first glimpse of my destination was a poignant moment of terrifying anticipation, for there, standing bold and awaiting was a place that bore, and still bears, a frightening and almost sinister resemblance to Alcatraz! In hindsight, I'd probably have been a lot happier had that in fact been the case.

Of all the questionings that abound in the world, one of the most unfailing and puzzling ones must surely be 'What moves people to willingly travel in their thousands to a place of such forlorn desolation to undertake one of the harshest pilgrimages in the world?' It's probably even more puzzling when you realise that people actually pay to do it! While one could be forgiven for believing that busy lives and changing social attitudes would have had a dramatic effect on visitors to Lough Derg, it is still an amazing monument to faith, religion or whatever, that so many thousands of people still go. Perhaps it's a case of the human form still needing something spiritual to cling to.

As with most people brought up in an urban setting, life will generally consist of the incessant hum of traffic and road works, the constant company of loud music blaring from shops and offices, and the general noise that goes with a large city environment. When you visit Lough Derg it takes a while to 'detox' and the withdrawals come in strange ways. While walking around the basilica on a long cold night reciting something akin to a mantra, it is not unusual to be suddenly overwhelmed with an urgent need to know what's going on in *Coronation Street, Brookside, Home & Away* or *Fair City*.

It is also quite normal to see what were once sane, sensible and immaculately groomed people looking like starving wrecks. They do tell you, of course, that this is just a temporary phase of detoxification and you feel wonderful afterwards. Thanks to this three-day adventure, I have also mastered the art of not alone falling asleep standing up, but staying asleep while walking around. The trick is the repetition of the 'Hail Mary'. This can be used very successfully for all insomniacs and saves a huge amount of visiting busy GP's!

Feeding times are interesting and after the initial shock you can even begin to look forward to them. The toast, while ok if it's hot with lashings of butter and marmalade on it, is a touch indigestible if eaten dry. The oat biscuits on the other hand, bear a striking resemblance in look, taste and consistency to the well-known building provision aeroboard, and to this day I am reluctant to let either oat biscuits or aeroboard inside the door of the house. Builders on the other hand are more than welcome if you can get one!

Day times in Lough Derg are busy and interesting and its true that the normal day-to-day problems that beset us mortals tend to fade into the background. The mind is clearly focused on other more pressing issues and, depending on the time you visit, the problems can vary in severity. Should you be blessed with good or reasonably good weather, most of the day is utilised swatting midges, the more you swat the higher the indulgence! These midges show no compassion and even fewer manners. They bite hard and relentlessly on faces, hands, arms, feet and any other bit of exposed flesh. On the other hand, should you be unfortunate enough to encounter adverse weather conditions, that's different. It would surely question Einstein's Theory of Relativity as to how simple rain and wind can sneak through the tightest hoods, the thickest jumpers, the warmest hats and the most waterproof trousers, to drip cold and uninvited, drop by drop down the back until it gets almost into the very bones. The one consolation is the fact that during this type of weather at least there aren't any midges, and I suppose you have to be thankful for small mercies!

On the third day, heading off the island, I have to concede that despite everything, you do get an enormous feeling of satisfaction. It's a strange feeling of calm and peace. This has absolutely nothing to do with the fact that the three days are over or the fact that you've just passed a boatload of pilgrims just beginning their visit!

Yes, I think everyone should do Lough Derg at least once. If nothing else, it's an escape from the constant hustle and bustle of everyday life where the mind can unfold and begin to think and, if you're a sceptic like me, you can always say you've done it to be on the safe side if nothing else! Doing Lough Derg does not label you a religious fanatic or anything remotely close and this is borne out by the huge cross-section of people from every walk of life who come each year in their thousands. Some, like myself, with understandable trepidation came for the first time, only to find they keep returning.

They say if you look back at the island from the boat something about this strange mystic place will keep drawing you back. I'm now happy to report that I've just purchased a blindfold!

Joe Toal

Leaving the sins behind

The first time I went on pilgrimage to Lough Derg in the mid-80s, I set off in the spirit of 'let's go and see what this is about', seeing it as something a bit off-beat or as a good topic of conversation in the future – 'O yes, I did Lough Derg once, and it was…' My motives for going were, therefore, a bit superficial – inquisitive rather than spiritual, although I was aware it would be quite a difficult place to live on for the days I would be there. I was in for a rude awakening. After the pleasant boat journey over, the visit to the dormitory (and the bed which when next I saw it would appear like a little piece of heaven on earth), and the leaving behind of my shoes and socks, I found myself a few minutes later at the cross on the wall of the church with arms outstretched repeating three times (at least) 'I renounce the world, the flesh and the devil.' I was really taken aback – did I want to do this? Did I really want to give up these things? Well, the devil, yes, but the world and the flesh … sometimes … maybe! It really hit me though that this was for real, that this was a place of testing, of giving up some of the comforts and things which I was too attached to and coming closer to God again. From that moment, throughout the following days, I discovered that the prayers and the penitential exercises of Lough Derg were not just a curiosity, but a real test of faith and an examination of one's life in the light of Christ's teaching. I think the spirit of the island touched me and told me this is not a place for messing around in, but rather of emptying yourself of sin and worldliness and of growing closer again to God.

I soon noticed I was sharing this experience with quite a number of other people. As each person had come as a penitent pilgrim, we were suffering together but also helping one another along the way. The patient following of one another around the penitential beds, each person saying their prayers privately yet sharing the same struggle to find a reasonable spot to step on next, somehow seemed to symbolise the struggle everyone has on the path of daily living. How often we need the example and support of those who walk before us and show us the way.

The night hours brought the vigil and the struggle to stay awake through the hours of darkness. The fact that we prayed together and that we again followed one another round the church as we made the night stations, brought encouragement and support when the cold began to seep in and tiredness lowered morale. One thought of those for whom the night-time is always an ordeal – those in pain, the lonely, the abandoned and the homeless; and one thought also of Christ and his hours of prayer to the Father in the darkness, and his own hours of pain and abandonment in the garden and on the cross.

The daylight brought new hope and the celebration of Mass. The priests present, who had been indistinguishable up until now from their fellow pilgrims, concelebrated Mass. Again one sensed in this group a spirit of being in something together, thankful to have survived the night and to have the privilege now of celebrating eucharist on St Patrick's island. As with the other services and prayer-times, simplicity and devotion seemed to be the key qualities emphasised during this liturgy.

The priests present were also asked to help out at the penitential service a little later on in the morning, when we were each given a position as confessor along the basilica sanctuary. I found this a moving and challenging experience. A number of the people who celebrated the sacrament with me had come to Lough Derg with difficult problems in their lives; sometimes things hidden in their lives for a great number of years. They hoped to find in this holy place something that would help them. I sensed that the opportunity to come to the sacrament of reconciliation was the moment they chose to come and place their lives before God, and through the ministry of the priest, to welcome the gift of Christ's forgiveness into their hearts. It struck me that, unlike myself, many people came to Lough Derg because they needed to find some answer or help for the difficulties they had in their lives, and that when they had participated in the spiritual and penitential exercises there, they received the grace of seeing themselves and their lives in a new light. They had great courage in coming and speaking to a priest in a very open manner in the sacrament of reconciliation. I felt very blessed to be able to hear these confessions – I can truly say I have rarely heard such honesty and openness in confessions elsewhere. From my experience, I really feel that what people come to Lough Derg for most of all is to be reconciled with God, to leave behind the failures and hurts of the past, to look to the future with great hope – to empty themselves of the world, the flesh and the devil, and to be filled once again with the love and grace of Jesus Christ through the power of the Holy Spirit. Also my own rather base and superficial motives for coming to Lough Derg were shown up to me for what they really were – a total misjudgement of what this place of testing, prayer and sacrifice could mean for the pilgrim who comes in the spirit of seeking God, being reconciled with him and leaving behind whatever is sinful in one's life.

Peter Tiernan

All of six decades

'Station Island' presents an intriguing sight from the shoreline of Lough Derg. There is the appearance of a green-domed basilica and adjoining buildings, so tightly clustered around it that they all seem to be floating on some miracle raft. It is difficult to imagine that they have any anchorage at all. And yet it is recorded that over 2000 pilgrims have been accommodated on this remarkable island at any one time. It is one of perhaps fifty other islands on Lough Derg, and it is not the largest. However, it is chosen for its association with St Patrick. Remarkable it is, because there it is as if time has stood still for the last sixteen hundred years. The Patrician age endures, where there is as much seclusion today as when St Patrick was attracted to its solitude. As for the landscape, it remains practically unaltered through the centuries.

What of the pilgrim exercises themselves? During the six decades that I have taken part, the faithfulness with which these exercises have been observed is quite impressive – three days fasting, virtually 36 hours without sleep, and in bare feet at that, enduring those century-old sharp stones, unsmoothed by the trafficking of hundreds of thousands of pilgrim feet and of course the night vigil, which challenges the will power of the most determined.

During my time on pilgrimage, perhaps the only concession to 'comfort' has been the concreting around the perimeter of the basilica. Even prior to this happening, I often wondered what forces impelled some pilgrims, especially on the ninth and final station, to circle the basilica at breakneck speed. At such speeds I still marvel how it is possible to recite seven decades of the

Rosary, together with the Creed, while circling the basilica just four times. Perhaps the repetition of the Hail Marys and Holy Marys over the previous days has developed a special skill. As some of these record breakers outpace me, my thoughts sometimes turn to St Paul in his letter to the Corinthians (and I promptly lose count of my Hail Marys!): 'Surely you know that many runners take part in a race but only one of them wins the prize. Run then in such a way as to win the prize.' Would this ever be the motivation?

Lough Derg is a great place to study feet; all shapes and sizes. As the rounds of the 'beds' are made, it is impossible not to notice as they curl and twitch over sharp and oft times wet stones. This is even truer in latter years (with reduced numbers in attendance) where a pilgrim may no longer 'enjoy' the support of a helping/restraining hand. Yes, these very feet are propelling us towards eternity as we make our stations – a fruitful subject for meditation.

Perhaps the vigil is the greatest challenge. That early morning Mass certainly does test the resoluteness of the most resolute. Before Vatican II, in the absence of concelebration, one way of overcoming that early sleep problem was by volunteering to serve the Masses of one or more of the pilgrim priests. Nowadays the only way I can think of reducing the risk of falling asleep, at a vulnerable time during the vigil, is to volunteer to lead a station. But of course the inherent risk, which is much greater during the night, is to omit a 'bed' or more likely to skimp on a Hail Mary or two!

What is it that brings pilgrims to this remote island? In the words of Alice Curtayne written fifty years ago:

The island of St Patrick's Purgatory stands in the mind of this generation as a kind of holy Hy-Brasil or Land of the Blessed. It offers a complete relief to modern conditions of living. It gives deliverance from the feverish bustle of a mechanised age. Time here loses its tyranny. Slaves of clock and calendar, who spent all their years 'clocking in', not only on their professional and business hours, but even on their very leisure

and their sleep, are here at last emancipated. This release
from the clutches of the clock hand gives a man freedom that
is so necessary for a spiritual adventure.

The pilgrim finds himself cloaked in the most complete
and reassuring anonymity. His name has been recorded,
true, but this is kept private. He puts his belongings in the
cubicle allotted to him and henceforth he is known only by
the number of that cubicle. He need reveal his name to no-
one unless he likes. He need converse with no-one unless by
choice ... When the newcomer casts off his footwear, it is a
symbol that he is shedding, at the same time, all those exter-
nals that make up status and lend importance to the individual: house family and dependants, atmosphere, daily occu-
pation. If he is a personage in his ordinary life, he undergoes
an immense levelling and becomes just one of the crowd.

One could not quibble with those sentiments. Or is there
something else, perhaps more fundamental still, which draws
pilgrims? Perhaps there is something indelible in the Irish psy-
che, born of sixteen centuries of observance, which explains the
phenomenon, because phenomenon it is. If this is so, then Lough
Derg will be there for another sixteen centuries. And, God willing, I will see a seventh decade on the Island!

Mary Thompson

An annual return

We all have certain 'constants' in our lives and Lough Derg is one such for me. Summer doesn't start until I have been to 'The Island'.

Thinking back, over at least thirty years, brings to mind the changes which have taken place. From the early days when queues and Lough Derg were synonymous, along with hard lumpy beds, black tea and the women's shelter with the turf fire, the accommodation is now luxurious. However, some things never change – the midges, cold and utter weariness! The harsh dictatorial attitude has given way to a more caring, inclusive approach.

Lough Derg conjures up many different images such as the physical discomforts and the heightened awareness of beauty in the sunsets and dawns and the time to really enjoy them. The people encountered on the island, from staff to pilgrims, play a pivotal role during the pilgrimage. The relevant and meaningful homilies – while one is still alert enough to appreciate them – the richness of the cantor's voice, the journeys and efforts undertaken by other pilgrims; all combine to influence the quality of the exercise.

I find that Lough Derg provides an excellent opportunity, which some of us need, to take a break from routine, get away from everything and try to be spiritual and contemplative for a few days. No guilt trip for that long weekend away!

The adverse conditions of hunger, cold and tiredness cannot take away the feeling of satisfaction and well-being there is on that final morning whilst waiting for the boat with shoes on.

Although I never make a promise to do it again, I subconsciously hope that my health permits and the compulsion is still on me for many years to come. There is that certain something about the place which pulls me back year after year.

Alice Taylor

from Tea and Toast

Women's liberation came to Lough Derg before it hit the main-land, because St Brigid is at the top here. You start with her and you must watch your step as she is extremely steep and you could break your neck if you decided to rush her. Next comes St Brendan, who is to her right and slightly lower down where she can keep an eye on him. He is rough and edgy with treacherous spiked stones that could penetrate a hastily positioned toe; the secret here is careful, premeditated movement. Then comes St Catherine, who has a pathway of small, sharp, cruel stones, and then Columba who is easier. Next is St Patrick and finally the double bed of Davog and Molaise who, maybe because double beds are conducive to relaxation, lie in flat comfort under an overhanging tree on the water's edge. These little beds have lain here for centuries and thousands of barefoot pilgrims have walked and prayed over them. Sometimes the prayers are pep-pered with unpremeditated swearing as the bitter little stones extract their last drop of penitential hardship.

The variety of feet on Lough Derg tell an interesting story. The soft perfectly formed feet of the very young flit over the stones like nimble hooves of mountain goats. Slightly older feet are still almost in their original condition, but are not quite as flexible on the rocks. Then come the older ones, branching out like gnarled trees into mature humps and bumps. But very old feet, like very old faces, are the most fascinating of all. They are like craggy rocks, some distorted into unusual shapes with var-ied toe formations and discoloured toenails. All these feet move over the beds, clambering, slipping, climbing and seeking level footholds. Some toes are bandaged and the most touching sight of all are the feet of women, no longer young, wearing elastic stockings which are covered at the heel with wet mud. The feet of Lough Derg are a touching, impressive sight. Sometimes when the strong, bony toe of a mountainy man cracks against a spiked rock, a few extra prayers are said that were never heard in church! Here in Lough Derg is a hidden core of our life that is difficult to analyse. It is as Irish as the brown bogs and grey mountains and is a living, breathing essence that still runs through our veins.

Lough Derg possesses a deep quietness. The sounds to be heard are the lapping of lake water against rocks, the murmur of voices and occasional birdsong. No footsteps disturb the stillness. Transistors, televisions, phones and cameras are not allowed to intrude here. You are without shoes, without food, without sleep and in the monotonous repetition of prayers, your mind is cleansed of all thoughts. Here your outer layers are stripped off. Your mind is cleared of clutter and you set aside all the things that were so important on the mainland. You have stepped off the world for two days and Lough Derg removes the dead layers of mental debris. It happens almost without your awareness, and as the second day draws to a close, you find an inner peace seeping into your being. If you so desire, you can chat to different people. Many come back again and again, finding here something that defies analysis. Maybe it is time out of life.

The accents of every county mingle together and indeed some not Irish. In the basilica I looked at all the different faces and wondered what kind of person came here, but there was no answer. The very old stun you with their tenacity; men and women with faces like hewn rocks; country people who have worked hard and prayed well all their lives. Others with golden, even tans acquired in warmer climates grip the rocks with well-manicured, multi-ringed fingers. Students imploring God for merciful examiners struggle with their first experience of exposure to cold and hunger. The young, the old, the middle-aged, from all walks of life, come to Lough Derg. We went home with quiet pools of peace in our hearts, a peace formed in the long hours away from the normal world.

Alice Taylor

Needs

Give me space
To roll out my mind,
So that I can open
The locked corners
Where lost thoughts
Are hidden.
I need time
In a quiet place
To walk around
The outer edges
Of my being,
To pick up
Fragmented pieces,
To put myself
Back together again.

Jim Snow

Years of service

I worked for fifty-three years on Lough Derg. I started on 2 May 1942 and retired on 22 December 1995. In the early days we worked a fifty-hour week, starting at 8.00 every morning and worked until 6 o'clock. We had an hour for dinner at 1 o'clock and that was the only break we got. Conditions became much better in recent years, with the new boats and shorter working hours.

I took charge of the boats in 1967. Before that Tommy Flood, who had taken over from his father, Johnny, was in charge of them. At that time there were up to twenty men employed on the boats compared to only five or six now. Motor boats were first used in the 1948 season. Before that the boats were all rowed with four to six men on each oar. Depending on the weather conditions, the crossing could take between ten minutes and an hour.

As a Lough Derg boatman, I can honestly say that I enjoyed the company of any man I ever worked with. I never had a problem with any of the men and I actually felt sad at the end of the season. Men like Willie Kane and Packie McGrath (Sarah-Ann) were great men to work with. The winters were always very long and often lonely with only myself and Jamsie Monaghan on the island. I might be working in the boathouse repairing or maintaining the boats and Jamsie would be out about the island doing various jobs and we would only see each other at lunch time. We were glad when the new season came.

I remember during the time when Mgr Flood was Prior, one day a bus load arrived from UCD. Several of the girls on the bus were wearing trousers which were not allowed. Girls were not permitted to wear trousers on the island! It was my job to make sure that any pilgrim going onto the island was properly dressed and so I insisted that they would have to change. It took a long time to persuade them but after a long argument with the chaplain they did go into the ladies to change. However when they arrived at the boat they were all wearing very short mini-skirts – sure that was far worse! But I had to let them go on.

I remember three deaths during my time on the island. In the early 1950s a Scottish dentist came on pilgrimage with his mother and died of a heart attack. He was buried in Pettigo.

On another occasion a Dublin man was in the queue outside St Mary's waiting for the boat when he collapsed and died. By a strange coincidence that man's daughter had arrived on pilgrimage the previous day, neither knowing the other was there. She then went back to Dublin with his remains.

The third man was from Carrick-on-Shannon in Co Leitrim. He was sitting on one of the benches in the sun chatting to a doctor when he suddenly fell over and died.

One very wet day an unfortunate lady fell and broke her leg. I was sent for to get her to the boat on the chair so that she could be taken to hospital. As we were getting her ready to go wasn't another lady carried in to First Aid who had also fallen and broken her leg. Both of them were taken to the Erne hospital in Enniskillen in the same car!

On another occasion an inspector from the Department of the Marine came to inspect the boats. It was a Sunday and he had brought his wife with him who was a nurse. After completing his work we were walking back down the island when he slipped and fell and broke his leg. We rolled him onto a big flat board and carried him to the boat and then to the car and his wife took him to Sligo hospital. We got a lovely letter from him afterwards thanking us for all our help.

I did the pilgrimage myself, twelve times in all. I think it was worse on those of us who work in the place because we know every stone so well. Six or seven of us workmen used to do it together. When we finished the pilgrimage we would cycle to

Sligo, stay there overnight and then cycle on to Mayo and climb Croagh Patrick.

In my 29 years as Boatman I only missed one day from work during the pilgrimage season and that was for my uncle's funeral in Dublin. I used to stay on the island every night of the season from 1 June till 15 August. Jamsie used to do one night a week if I wanted a night off.

During those years over 600,000 pilgrims were ferried across the lake and I take a certain satisfaction in the fact that not one pilgrim was ever hurt or injured on the boats. Safety was always important with us. We had very skilled drivers too. There was a lot more skill needed for the rowing boats than for the motor boats. You had to depend on the wind and the driver's skill to stop the rowing boat at the pier whereas you just put the motor boat into reverse and it stops very easily. We always had a system for the boats when the pilgrims were going home. First we would fill the St Columba on one side of the pier and it would go off. Then we would fill the St Patrick which held 100 passengers and had to be towed by the small St Brigid. This meant that the crew of the Columba would reach the shore first, get their boat unloaded and then be there to help to 'land' the big boat to ensure everyone's safety. The Patrick was still being rowed when I took over the boats in 1967 but we stopped rowing it a year or two later. It was a tough job rowing – you had to stand up to row the Patrick.

When I retired I got a lovely piece of Tyrone Crystal with the St Brendan boat engraved on it – that was the boat I was most closely associated with. I enjoyed every minute I worked on Lough Derg. Because life is at stake where a boat is concerned, the well-being of passengers and crew must be the main concern of any boatman. In my retirement I am happy knowing that my half-century's work and more at Lough Derg was always done to the best of my ability.

John Sherrington

The danger of false expectations

'You have made a very general confession. Is there anything troubling you that you would like to leave behind on the island? I do not want you to go home and regret not having left behind a burden from the past.' I have often reflected on these words which I used in confession during my pilgrimage to Lough Derg. They were not prepared; intuitively on the Sunday morning listening to a penitent's confession against the background murmur of repentant voices kneeling at the altar rails, I asked this question. The woman unburdened the sin that had troubled her for many years and like the woman bent-double, she straightened up and left at peace with God (Lk 13:11).

Thirteen centuries earlier, the abbot, Cummean (c. 650 AD), founder of a monastery at Kilcummin, and maybe associated with the monastery at Clonfert, had commenced his Penitential Book with an introductory sentence which expressed that its purpose was to provide 'health-giving medicine of souls'. The link between these two events is the psychological need to express our wrongdoing to another person and be accepted, and the spiritual need to ask for forgiveness of sin. The penitents on pilgrimage are a reminder of the deep human need to express one's deepest self and be accepted by another person who mediates God's presence. The dark, shadowy, hidden actions of life need to be healed for health and life. Ignored or pushed down under the calm, collected face of efficiency, they rage and oppress the fragile spirit.

A moment of grace and a reminder of God's mysterious dealings with each precious life. At the end of an eight year period of teaching in Ireland, I decided that part of my leaving would be a pilgrimage of thanksgiving to Lough Derg. As an Englishman living in Dublin, I realised how much I had learnt about the painful relationship between the two islands, which are physically so close and yet so distant. A pilgrimage of thanksgiving and prayer for peace motivated me to the island. Two of us crossed together to the island, a man from the North and myself. Confused by the language of stations, the prayers and the rhythms of the day, he introduced me to the pattern of prayer. The afternoon was bright and it did not seem too hard. In the evening the priest introduced us to the theme of becoming still and centred. As we walked and prayed, the physical circling of the stations could lead to the stilling, perhaps at times the numbing, of the mind and then a glimpse or awareness of the life of the spirit. Our Father ... Hail Mary ... Hail Mary ... the mantra of the prayer seemed tedious and repetitive. I hoped for quick results; always the danger of an overactive mind.

The first night was wet and cold. The puddles on the stone flags were chilled by the bitter wind. I was miserable and I cursed the decision to come here. I waited for the dawn; a bright dawn with the appearance of the sun would break this cold vigil and be a sign of new life. Optimistic thoughts, and evermore imaginative thoughts ... All mirages as the weak daylight desperately tried to break into the night. It continued to rain. It was a chill, grey dawn revealing a sky full of heavily-laden rain clouds. I have often reflected on that dawn. Perhaps at Lough Derg, I learnt a little more of the need to live the reality of life – what is real and needs to be faced; how often do I live in the cloud of unreality, the imagined, the hoped-for and therefore fail to recognise the real about me? Optimism, a vague, unreal thought needs to be replaced by hope. The future can be different, but I cannot control it or demand it. It is a reminder that however much humans or religions might try to control God, it is impossible. God's ways are not our ways. Humility follows.

As hour followed hour on a long Saturday afternoon, prayer followed prayer, and battle was fought with tiredness. When should I drink black tea and eat toast became the preoccupying question. Looking back on the afternoon, it taught me the importance of waiting. In an instant society and e-mail culture, waiting is difficult. Like the potter at the wheel, God is the slowest of workers. The moulding of the human spirit cannot be done violently; rather it requires time and gentle caressing, otherwise the spirit will be crushed. With contemporary focus on an emotional experience of God, prayer can become the hope for a good feeling. The mystics remind seekers of God that much prayer is spent in darkness or in the cloud of unknowing. The invitation is to be patient and wait in hope.

Dead tired, the bunkbed was sheer bliss. I awoke to brilliant sunlight spilling into the room. The unexpected broke into the expected gloom. Sheer gift. The light bounced off the stones and reflected from the gentle waves as they rippled upon the shore. Joy was accompanied by a sense of peace. From the depths of the heart there arose a hymn of praise. The pattern of walking in circles had spiralled my mind inwards to the heart and the sanctuary where God is encountered. In that moment, the words 'I did not call the virtuous but sinners' revealed the God who is merciful and desires mercy. A fleeting moment and it passed.

On the morning of resurrection, the angel told the women, 'He is going before you to Galilee; it is there you will see him, just as he told you' (Mk 16:8). Our Galilee is found in everyday life, in the midst of the routines and familiar patterns of life. There, in faith, the Risen Christ is encountered. The High Cross of Monasterboice depicts the story of the last Judgement and reminds those who come to the graveyard that God is loved through the love of neighbour: 'in so far as you did this to one of the least of these, you did it to me' (Mt 25:40).

Three days of pilgrimage broke my false expectations. They were shown to be the illusion which they are. Through the journey of circling, the rain, the cold and the sun, hope was nurtured that God's blessing continues to break into life, often in strange and unexpected ways. Hope renews faith. Lough Derg is a reminder to one pilgrim that the Celtic mystery of life needs to confront his Anglo-Saxon pragmatism.

Peter Raftery

Island vigil

No matter how often a pilgrim has undertaken the Lough Derg pilgrimage, there is always a sense of anticipation, of expectancy, and of muted excitement during the intervening hour between the end of night prayer and the beginning of the vigil. Certain practical details have to be seen to – rain coats, warm sweaters, bottles of water are among the various items that have to be retrieved from the hostel and deposited in the Night Shelters lest the night turn out to be cold and wet. A sense of serenity and calm begins to descend on the island. If it has been a sunny day, those who have their preparations completed can spend a few minutes marvelling at the splendour of the stained glass windows in the basilica as their shining colours come to life in the light of the setting sun. There is an opportunity to stand at the western wall behind the basilica and look out over the placid waters of the lake as countless pilgrims over the centuries have done.

The solemn closing of the basilica doors by two of the pilgrims is a tangible sign that the Vigil is about to begin and recalls the medieval practice which saw the pilgrims of that time enter the cave to begin a vigil, not of twenty-four hours but of anything up to fifteen days. The solemn lighting of the vigil candle never loses its significance, even though the lighting takes place every evening during the pilgrimage season. For each succeeding group of pilgrims, it is a timeless symbol of the presence among them of Christ, the light of the world with whom they are keeping watch during the hours of darkness – just as he so often did during his life on earth, culminating in the great vigil he kept on the night before he died as he suffered his agony in the Garden of Olives.

By keeping vigil, the Lough Derg pilgrims are giving human expression to one of the deepest realities of the Christian faith. By keeping watch during the hours of darkness, and by not sleeping, the pilgrims are saying not so much in words as in deeds that they believe that when our journey of life is over, we will pass from life to life without submitting to the darkness of endless death. The pilgrim sees the darkness of the night give way to the splendour of the dawn which is itself a potent symbol of the resurrection.

Reconciliation is at the heart of Lough Derg. Christ by his death and resurrection has reconciled us to the Father. The medieval Easter hymn *Victimae Paschali* expresses it as *Agnus redemit oves* – 'the lamb has redeemed the sheep'. The recalling in spirit, mind and body of that death and resurrection is at the heart of the Lough Derg Vigil.

Patricia Olivier

Light out of darkness

I am sure I went to Lough Derg initially because my name is Patricia; as when I converted back to God in 1980 I said spontaneously that day a prayer which five years later I discovered to be St Patrick's Breastplate. So, when I read an article one day in a magazine about the pilgrimage to St Patrick's Purgatory, I thought: 'One day I will go.' Four years later I still had not made the decision to go but that year my daughter Audrey had died in a car crash. She was eighteen years old, she was the jewel of my heart, she was the beauty in my life. This made me decide to go to Lough Derg the following June.

I thought I was strong. I had coped with my bereavement as well as could be expected, due only to my great faith. But on the morning of the confession I burst into tears. I could feel the terrible weight of the sins of my life so heavy, I was exhausted and felt no hope was possible. It was then a priest took me in his arms and said 'but don't forget that God loves you and all through your life you will be able to say to him "sorry my God, so sorry my God".' It was then I received an enlightenment, almost like the cork of a champagne bottle popping. Joy was flowing plentifully. I realised that all my life I could say 'Sorry my God'. Instantly I felt myself part of God just like the prodigal son found again and saved. On leaving this pilgrimage I felt completely shattered, physically exhausted but also as 'white as snow'.

As well as all this, I had the immense joy of meeting the Irish people and experiencing their kindness. Before going I imagined the pilgrimage being rather cosmopolitan but in fact it was very Irish, which made it even more engaging as I was able to understand the devotion and closeness of the Irish people to the Lord Jesus and to St Patrick.

Despite the hardship encountered during the pilgrimage, I hope to go back. Thanks to all those I met there.

David Meadon

Cradle of Celtic Christianity

Summing up my first experience of St Patrick's Purgatory at Lough Derg in a few words is not easy. Reflecting, with the benefit of eighteen months hindsight, the strongest memory I have is that of praying the stations in the basilica during the night of the vigil. There was something very tangible, a real meeting of earth and heaven as, barefooted, we padded around together, to the intonation of the rosary. Prayer so often seems a solitary experience, even in church, surrounded by others. Yet at Lough Derg that night, for me there was a real sense of unity. Yes we were individuals but we prayed the same prayers and somehow we were one, much more so even than earlier in the day as we picked our way over the uneven stones surrounding the cells. It was the most positive experience of Christian unity that I have personally experienced and it was somehow appropriate that it should be in Ireland, that cradle of Celtic Christianity.

It was the more poignant for me, having been brought up in the Anglican (Church of England) tradition, but who came seeking to find an answer as to whether to convert to the church of Rome. During the prayers that night it mattered not. My brother and sister pilgrims accepted me and I them; and God accepted us all.

St Patrick's Purgatory is not easy, but we are told the best things in life never are. The first experience may well be the easiest, as you never really know what to expect. Next time may well be different. I am grateful to the friend and her family who invited me, and with whom I shared the experience. There is nothing to my knowledge comparable within the Anglican Church. Yet there is much to gain, once you force yourself to go beyond the painful feet, the midges and the physical hunger. Between the prayers and the various services in the basilica, there is much time for reflection and just as importantly for talk. How often do we really talk to friends and families these days? Not much perhaps and even less on spiritual matters.

Time too for personal prayers which for me were important just at that time, as a close friend suffered the anguish of watching her mother decline into a terminal illness. Prayer had for me become, I must admit, a perfunctory exercise, so going to Lough Derg meant a challenge. It was another positive aspect to feel so many of my prayers were answered in the months that followed.

And no, it wasn't all easy or straightforward. I found it hard to accept that the Irish could pray so rapidly when it took me so long. It wasn't until I talked about this to one of the sisters that I was able to accept that speed was unimportant – it was, as they say, the thought that counts! I later found that praying faster concentrated the mind much more – fewer opportunities to be diverted by other thoughts.

So will I return? I hope so. It's said that if you look back at the island as you leave on the boat, you will return. I had a good long look. I would be sad if I did not get the opportunity to go back. There is much to gain amidst the personal hardship; gains that neither time nor moth can destroy.

Gerard Mc Sorley

The renovation programme of the 1980s

Mention Lough Derg and thoughts of fasting, prayer, sore feet and black tea spring to mind. In the 1980s a new topic of conversation became part of the Lough Derg scene. Talk of renovation and fund-raising filled the air, for it was in this decade that a major building programme commenced on the Island. It had been twenty-five years since any major construction had taken place when the men's hospice was extended and a new staff residence erected to replace the old one, so beloved by pilgrims who waited at St Mary's for early morning confession.

All buildings on Lough Derg suffer greatly in the harsh winter conditions associated with its island location. In 1980 it was obvious that serious repair work needed to be embarked upon. Erosion was extensive in buildings and walls close to the water's edge, while the women's hospice showed serious signs of deterioration.

As a first step, it was decided to have a survey done of all the island facilities. Mr Joseph Tracey of the firm of architects, McCormick, Tracey & Mullarkey of Derry, was instructed to carry out a complete inspection in the autumn of 1980. His initial report confirmed the worst suspicions. The two piers on the mainland and island needed urgent attention. The platform surrounding St Patrick's Basilica showed serious erosion both on the underside and topside. But it was the women's hospice which gave rise to most concern. It was built in the early 1900s to accommodate 600 beds, kitchen and laundry facilities. In 1935 the foundation had moved slightly and steel girders were erected throughout the building to support it. These had eroded. Added to these problems was the fact that the building did not conform to the safety regulations of the 1980s. Erection of fire escapes and other alterations would result in a considerable loss in accommodation space. There were two options – repair the building and still be left with an old building or build a new one on a new site. A rough costing of both options showed it would take approximately £1million to repair the present building and £2.5 million to build a new one. Either way, large sums of money were involved.

In 1981 Mr Tracey was instructed to draw up plans for a new hospice on a site to be reclaimed from the lake. He had already retained Thomas Garland and Partners, Dublin, Civil Engineers, and now Mr Denis Lavelle & Associates, Service Consultants, Holywood, Co Down were added to his team. As the plans and consultations progressed, it became clear that the cost of the new building would exceed £3million. Should the project go ahead? Early in 1983, at a meeting in the Bishop's House, Monaghan, it was decided to proceed. This decision was really an act of faith in the pilgrimage itself and especially in the generosity of the thousands of pilgrims who had made the pilgrimage in the past and would continue to do in the future. As events unfolded, this act of faith was not misplaced.

Work on other areas of concern was already in progress. Under the guidance of Mr John Gwynn of Thomas Garland & Partners, the two piers were repaired by Joseph McMenamin & Co, Donegal in 1981-2. The topside of the basilica platform was repaired by City Asphalt, Derry and by Thomas Martin & Son, Pettigo, in 1982-3. The underside of the platform and the foundations exposed to water proved a more difficult project due to lack of space when the water level was high. Eventually it was to be completed by P. J. Edwards & Co Ltd, Dublin in 1984-5.

The contract for the new hospice went to tender early in 1984 and it was awarded to Messrs McAleer & Teague, Building Contractors, Dromore, Co Tyrone, at a figure of £3.5million. Work began on reclaiming the site in May of that year. Actual building started in 1985. The building of this new hospice, together with the raising of the necessary finance, remains one of the minor miracles of Lough Derg's history. So many things fell readily into place that it was obvious that a guiding hand was directing the operation.

The site for the new hospice, with its shallow depth of water and rock foundation, together with its position in relation to other buildings on the island, fitted in nicely to Lough Derg requirements. The ferrying of materials, which was initially perceived as a major problem, worked smoothly over the three years of construction work. Even the weather conspired to be of assistance. No major storms occurred. The project was blessed in having as its building contractors Messrs McAleer & Teague. They deserve the highest praise for the quality of their work and the speed of construction and for staying within the initial budget of £3.5million. However the highest accolade has to go to Mr Joseph Tracey and his team who masterminded the project. They can be justly proud of a magnificent achievement in extremely difficult circumstances. The new hospice, with its blend of ancient and modern, is a lasting tribute to Mr Tracey and his architectural expertise.

The funding of the project was another miracle. £3.5million was a daunting figure to raise. But with God, all things are possible.

Carr Communications of Dublin were retained to generate public interest in the project and the fund-raising was officially launched on 17 May 1983 in the Shelbourne Hotel, Dublin. It was clear from the beginning that no grants were available nor was big business interested in what was being done on Lough Derg. The funding of the project would depend on the ordinary pilgrim. How magnificently they responded. Small sums, large sums began to appear. From the day a parcel containing £3,580 arrived by post to the Lough Derg Fund, with no identification of the donor, it was clear that the guiding hand was at work. Also the publicity generated to raise the funds had the effect of highlighting the pilgrimage itself. The number of pilgrims rose from 17,000 in 1980 to almost 30,000 in 1988. On the banking scene, the interest rates were high when money was on deposit in 1984 and they had dropped considerably by the time borrowing was needed. At no time did the building programme interfere with the annual pilgrimage. Indeed so many things conspired to bring the renovation programme to a successful conclusion that it is obvious God had a huge say in what took place.

In 1987-88 the sanctuary of St Patrick's Basilica was enlarged and refurbished. The work of building and renovating still continues under the capable hands of Mgr Richard Mohan and Mr Joseph Tracey. Much has been achieved since, but that is another story.

Two significant dates are associated with the 1980s on Lough Derg. The blessing and laying of the foundation stone of the new hospice by Most Rev Joseph Duffy, Bishop of Clogher, on 6 June 1986, and the blessing of the new hospice and dedication of the new Altar in St Patrick's Basilica by Bishop Duffy on 22 May, 1988, in the presence of Cardinal Tomás Ó Fiaich and other Church and State dignitaries.

As I reflect on the 1980s on Lough Derg, I thank God for the privilege of being associated with all that took place in those years. I thank Bishop Joseph Duffy for his unswerving support, and the staff on Lough Derg, clerical and lay, for their unstinting encouragement. But it is for the thousands of pilgrims, who were so generous in their giving, that I reserve my special thanks. They are the unsung heroes of St Patrick's Purgatory. Without their support the work would not have been done. May they be amply rewarded for their generosity.

Shaun McGregor

The mental and physical exertions

When I first 'did the Lough' in the summer of 1983 I came totally unprepared, was 'foundered', appropriately soaked and, on that occasion, ultimately renewed on this physically, spiritually and mentally challenging place. The renewal was warranted as spirits were low following the tragic death of my brother Paddy in May of 83. I was also very conscious of the fact that he had asked me to accompany him on the Lough Derg pilgrimage on the previous year. I had refused his offer in unambivalent and expletive terms! Now I, with my brothers, found myself there to honour his memory and come to terms with his loss. That visit in 1983 opened up a relationship with Lough Derg which continues to the present time.

The first visit to Lough Derg for the unseasoned pilgrim is too difficult to even begin to explain. A good day quickens the pulse and excites expectations; that is until jagged stones of St Brigid's and St Brendan's Beds make social acquaintances with the feet and toes! Sometimes the Hail Marys don't follow in sequence if the big toe gets jammed or scratched. A wet day simply demands more caution and care as well as coming to terms with the misery of the experience. Of course new pilgrims sometimes show an unhealthy disregard for more elderly folk who sometimes appear to 'dawdle' around the beds and hold everyone up. The seasoned observer has witnessed and experienced all this before and therefore tries to find balance to the pilgrimage exercises.

The weather has a profound impact on any sense of fashion on Lough Derg. Pilgrims very quickly adapt to both a unique, personal and shared, experience of real humility where the material world takes a back seat. Adapting to weather patterns may demand much more clothing than is normally worn, more insect repellent than is necessary or, in the case of hot weather, anything that protects against the sun. You can't win, and perhaps that is the essence of the 'Purgatory' experience.

In June 1984 I brought twenty-five fourth year pupils from Holy Cross College, Cookstown, to Lough Derg for the three-day pilgrimage. This was a gamble because the acknowledged demands and rigours of the pilgrimage were coupled with the vibrancy and energies of youth. To say that this was different to their normal daily experience was understatement personified. Yet, they responded magnificently and encouraged many adult pilgrims with their enthusiasm. Such was the success that the Lough Derg Pilgrimage became an annual school event. I will always remember with fondness and a great pride my association with those young people. I pay homage to their efforts. I profoundly believe that young people, if properly motivated, have so much to offer in maintaining the traditions of the Lough Derg Pilgrimage.

While constantly trying to promote it, I have neither adequately described, nor been able to explain, Lough Derg. This statement may sound paradoxical but it nevertheless is true. Lough Derg is an enigma with her own secrets and magnetism. To watch people struggle in barefoot humility, fasting, depriving self of sleep and engaging in an endless mantra of variable prayer, surely challenges the soul of the 'Why?' concept. There are countless reasons, as there are grains of sand, why pilgrims do this and they are all legitimate. No-one has a monopoly on reason and yet a peaceful tranquillity pervades the whole island.

Lough Derg humour is totally unique – the experience lends itself to unusual witness of funny situations which take nothing away from the spiritual experience. In many cases they add to it. It is a great place for real laughter without pretence or prompt. This humour is very reassuring amid an incredible pilgrim relationship which only they can identify with. Granted, many do not laugh and simply want to go home. While the use of the words 'Lough Derg meal' have a comic undertone, very few refuse to replenish lost energy with dry toast and milkless tea. Never, particularly in the company of young people, have I witnessed toast disappear so fast! Ample evidence of sleepwalking can be witnessed during the night of the vigil. People struggling to stay awake can unwittingly amuse others.

However, there is no real humour in trying to kill time! On Lough Derg, time is a powerful symbol. While water is the umbilical cord to the mainland it serves also to keep the pilgrim from the material world. Away from the pace of the material world one becomes aware of self … time allows that. The word 'Purgatory' demands that I give something in order to get something. I have plenty of time to give attention to the basic exercises of the pilgrimage. I also have plenty of time to get an assessment of where I am at, or what I want from life. The Lough Derg Pilgrimage allows me the opportunity to self-evaluate, to reflect and to renew. Back on the mainland it is much more difficult to be sensible but who knows what benefits are reaped from the pilgrimage? The absolute sense of relief in getting off the island also carries a sense of achievement and attainment. A feel good factor exists. To paraphrase the words of a Van Morrison song, 'it would be great if it was like this all the time'.

After a few visits to Lough Derg, one can make other observations; e.g. it is not always 'cool' to be a member of the island staff. They are not necessarily the free souls that pilgrims take them to be. Many undergo the 'island experience' every day of their 4-6 week stint in challenging circumstances. It is fairly evident at times that a week's rest would be graciously grabbed! I suppose the enclosed space of a small island over that period of time would bring it's own stresses.

The physical changes on the island over the quite recent past are commendable and a testament to the hard work and effort of the Prior and his team. One very noticeable feature is the increased number of journalists and photographers in evidence on the island at various times. In essence, there is nothing wrong with this as long as the pilgrims' efforts are not hindered.

However, it is unfair to everyone if reporting is negative, cynical or prejudicial. One must have a degree of sympathy for the Prior in relation to sanctioning journalistic visits. He cannot win.

Many people in the past few years have been pass remarkable as to reasons why pilgrim attendances rise or fall. I have given up on arguments, as I believe that the spiritual ethos of Lough Derg will look after itself. I intend to be a pilgrim as long as I am physically and mentally allowed to be so.

Shaun McGregor

The Night vigil

When a pebble becomes a boulder
And a foot unsure without a sock
When an insect becomes a dragon
And a stone becomes a rock.

When a breeze becomes a hurricane
And legs become molten lead
When prayer booms to the ceiling
And others asleep in bed.

When the cold becomes an iceberg
And arms dangled without grace
When the walking becomes a ritual
And night holds her regular face.

When dawn becomes a desire
And light a gracious relief
When spirituality becomes an awareness
And redemption a hidden belief.

When fog bounces gently on water
And a sigh comes with no deceit
When reality is totally appealing
And the night-time vigil is complete.

When Lough Derg unfolds her mystery
And challenges the very heart
The day doesn't appear so long now
After a long and painful start.

Fiona McGrath

Some memories
from behind the scenes

Having watched the boat cross over from the mainland carrying its precious cargo, they strained to see the safe arrival of the new recruit – with enough baggage to last the summer and well beyond. Then they waited on a June Sunday afternoon – mother and father, man and wife together, praying she'd be happy and settle in and maybe even enjoy herself. They stayed near the pier for a long time but eventually moved away, travelling long-forgotten by-roads that took them round the perimeter of the lake, all the time looking over at the drab greyness of it all for some sign of her returning – having beaten a hasty retreat! And who might blame a quiet sixteen-year-old for changing her mind and jumping ship from St Patrick's Purgatory, having accepted the offer of a summer's work miles from home? Despite their misgivings, she persevered that summer and many more besides.

That first journey to Lough Derg was often talked about in our house, especially as over the following decade it became as much a part of my student summers as J1 visas were to the majority of my counterparts. The island became a home from home, its workers an extended family and its pilgrims a source of knowledge and inspiration, occasional exasperation and frequent amusement.

My Lough Derg memories come first and foremost from an employee's point of view as it is in that role that I spent the most time there. Summers spent working to the rhythm of the pilgrimage were opportunities for growth and confidence building and despite the inevitable minor in-house squabbles, were ultimately very positive experiences.

Initially I found the work regime stark, with rising to the 6 am bell being the greatest penance of all. Making beds in the early morning when pilgrims were at Mass was a regimental team exercise carried out with little enthusiasm – especially if we'd stayed up late the night before! Dormitory accommodation did little for those who needed plenty of sleep. Everyone was awake until the night owls came home to roost or until the silent arrival of one of 'the sisters' put paid to any further teenage high jinx.

Despite the fairly disciplined timetable to which we worked, the island and all its summer inhabitants often provided distractions or diversions to occupy our minds if the routine ever threatened to be monotonous.

I clearly remember being drawn out onto the fire escape at the back of the old ladies' hostel around 7 am one Sunday morning by the sound of an army helicopter landing on the mainland. The noise carried over the water and was so loud at that early hour that it was decidedly intimidating. Being in such an isolated location, surrounded by forestry and close to the border, the island occasionally featured in security checks.

My first real experience of the effects of sunstroke also presented itself in a dawn bed-making session, when a fellow worker collapsed and required medical attention having fallen asleep in the sun the previous day and ending up looking like a lobster – well done on one side!

Occasionally the pilgrims unintentionally caused a stir – the lost bag, the boat missed, the number of visits in a season, the serious injury or even death.

One group of young men didn't quite embrace the spirit of the pilgrimage when they smuggled contraband onto the island and proceeded to consume it in the dormitories on their first night. The ensuing mayhem led to the discovery of a bottle of vodka dumped at the back of the shop, following a search by staff. The culprits were duly despatched to the mainland and calm was restored.

Pilgrims to the island were often inquisitive about what the workers got to eat – but largely just to occupy their minds on the second day of pilgrimage. After a night without sleep the slightest tit-bit of information or the waft of cooking smells from the staff quarters can be mind boggling. My own memories of meal times are of plenty of noise, wisecracks and occasional rows – especially when it came to washing up. In the early years the menus were predictable, based on the days of the week. Some of us abstained on a Tuesday when stew and tapioca were the offerings (what pilgrim wouldn't have gladly swapped places with us?) but looked forward to Sunday when ice cream was brought in from Pettigo after morning Mass.

I can recall the hype and excitement among the teenage workforce in the weeks prior to the marriage of Charles and Diana in July of 1981 and the scramble for places around the television set when the big day finally arrived. Having minimal contact with the outside world and few sources of entertainment, heightened our thirst for the 'glamour' that Lough Derg couldn't provide. That being said, the isolation also forced us to look within ourselves and to our peers for the strength and support that was needed to carry out our work and to get on with each other in the somewhat unnatural environment in which we found ourselves. As a result some strong and lasting friendships built up among us.

Rare visits to the island by the media were unsettling occasions. Individual reporters or film/photographic crews were granted entry on the basis that they experience the pilgrimage for themselves, yet they never really fitted in. Their presence seemed to make pilgrims wary and sometimes resentful as the uninitiated looked on with wonder or incredulity. Inevitably these visitors left early!

I first undertook the pilgrimage the second summer that I worked on Lough Derg – starting and finishing on the island, returning immediately to work the next day. This initial experience was largely to stem my curiosity as to what the place was all about. It was the beginning of a trend that has yet to be broken, as an annual return has become the norm.

In the mid to late 1980s many changes came about – not only in conditions for staff but also in the physical landscape of the island itself. This period will surely go down in the history of Lough Derg as a time of inspired development that saw the completion of the new ladies' hostel with all its associated facilities and the general upgrading of all pilgrim accommodation. As the pilgrims enjoyed the central heating, new bunks and a drying room, long-stay staff revelled in having access to a modern laundry with its washing machines and tumble dryers.

The introduction of coffee to the pilgrims' meagre menu was a godsend for those who couldn't face black tea. However, despite the improvements in comfort, safety and aesthetics, there was little change in the pilgrimage itself and none was expected. The station continues to follow the format handed down through the centuries from our forefathers to our present generation. I suspect that any suggestion of changing the traditional pilgrimage would be strongly rejected by those who presently support and love Lough Derg – the caretakers of its future.

In this consumer society of the Celtic Tiger many may have forgotten about nurturing the spirit. As Patrick Kavanagh so appropriately put it in the opening lines of his poem *Advent:*

We have tested and tasted too much, lover –
Through a chink too wide there comes in no wonder'

Perhaps all too soon society will be seeking sustenance that money cannot buy. Where better to refresh body, mind and soul than an isolated island in south Donegal?

From Cavan and from Leitrim and from Mayo
From all the barefaced parishes where hills
Are perished noses running peaty water
They come to Lough Derg to fast and pray and beg.
From Lough Derg *by Patrick Kavanagh*

James McDonagh, Patrick & Charlie Ward

A bed in heaven

James McDonagh and Patrick and Charlie Ward are members of
a travelling community which settled in Coalisland in the 1970s.
Patrick and Charlie are brothers and live in a permanent site,
'An Tearmain' in the Glen area of Coalisland. James and his family live in a semi-detached house in Inishmore Heights. They are
all pupils of St Joseph's High School, Coalisland.

Both James and Charlie have been to St Patrick's Purgatory
on three occasions. It has been a tradition among the travelling
community to undertake the pilgrimage on a regular basis. The
boys feel it is a good thing to go and no pressure is put on them.
They make a conscious decision to participate. Charlie first went
when he was twelve years old. They have a variety of motives.
Charlie said he went to pray for others and to avoid bad luck. He
has heard it said that if you go three times there would be a bed
in heaven for you. James said the first time he went was to pray
for his cousin, a newly born baby who was very seriously ill.

They usually go with Charlie's grandmother, Ellen Ward.
Their parents go at different times.

All agreed that the pilgrimage is difficult but the easiest part
was the first day of the first visit because they were not aware of
what they had to face. The hardest part is the first night where
they had to stay up and walk round in their bare feet on the very
cold and difficult ground. Charlie says he prefers it when it rains
because it keeps the flies away. They found it difficult to concentrate at the 6.30am Mass. Charlie didn't seem to mind the hunger
and said he preferred not to eat anything. It was not the kind of
place that young people would mess about in because of the
prayerful atmosphere. James and Charlie spoke with great affec-
tion about a priest who looks like 'Fr Ted'.

They gave a variety of reasons as to what they had gained from their experience. Charlie said he felt good for having completed the pilgrimage and felt he was a better person for it. His conscience was much clearer after the experience. He enjoyed presenting the offertory gifts at Mass. James said he felt like a new person and said it was like talking to God. Charlie also said it gave him an idea of how Jesus suffered.

They all agreed they would go back again. They remembered the words of a priest on the boat back from the island that if you look back you will go back.

As told to their teacher, Mr Duffy, Vice Principal,
St Joseph's High School, Coalisland.

Sean McCague

Living the beatitudes

My first visual contact with Lough Derg was as acting taxi-driver for a neighbour. I was delivering pilgrims. I turned the vehicle and happily headed home. Two days later I was back to collect them and learned much regarding their trials and tribulations on 'the island'. It wasn't long until I returned.

There was a certain trepidation as I paid my money at the office and headed for the boat. I felt somewhat like a student leaving home pondering the uncertainties of future college days. Despite having read the leaflet and pieced together the stories of former pilgrims, I was apprehensive about what exactly lay before me. I tagged along with the 'old hands' who knew exactly what was before them.

The removal of the shoes and socks had a great levelling effect. Everyone was on the one road. Going around the beds for the first time, when energy levels were high, didn't seem such a chore. I was greatly humbled by the fact that many older, slower pilgrims were happily edging along in deep meditation – their moving lips and devoutly closed eyes displaying a sense of direct communication with the Father. I needed to concentrate more.

When I arrived at the cross on the Basilica wall, where pilgrims prayed with outstretched arms, I had mixed emotions. I had never been touched by the visible expressions of Charismatics. I felt distinctly awkward as I repeated the actions of those who had moved along before me. But suddenly I felt at one with all present. Here I could identify the message of the Beatitudes as everyone shared the common goal of seeking reconciliation.

The remainder of the pilgrimage was easy thereafter. It was

easier to focus on why I came and how I should maximise my relationship with my God. I had little difficulty with the famous cuisine and my journey through a sleepless night was shortened by the friendships made with people who previously had been nodding acquaintances.

The bond of Christian fellowship is much stronger on Lough Derg than in any other place of Retreat I have visited. As one pushes out the boat to the strains of *Hail Glorious St Patrick,* there is an inner happiness seldom experienced anywhere else – an enrichment which cannot be captured with pen and paper.

Anne Cassidy

A Memory in Photographs

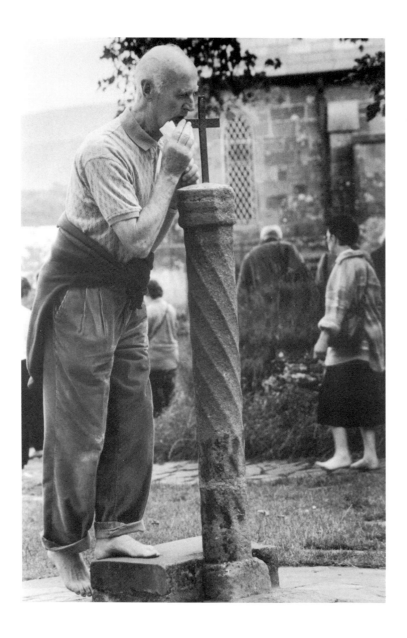

John McAreavey

A pilgrim among pilgrims

It would be easy at a distance of more than a hundred miles and about six months since my last Lough Derg pilgrimage, to be a little sentimental about it. That is something I do not want to do. But first, an introduction: in 1983, ten years after I was ordained, I went on pilgrimage to Lough Derg. For reasons that I cannot explain, I had resisted making the pilgrimage until then. Since then, I have made it each year. I have experienced Lough Derg only as a priest, so the view expressed here is a priest's view.

The first impression I have of the Lough Derg pilgrimage is that all pilgrims are equal. They are required to do the same exercises and in the same way. All differences of role are stripped away. What brings this home for me most clearly is being barefoot on the island. When we are stripped of that most basic protection, we are – literally – all on the same ground. The church teaches that 'flowing from their rebirth in Christ, there is a genuine equality of dignity and action among all of Christ's faithful'. This is not a part of the church's vision of herself that most Catholics would recognise. The Lough Derg pilgrimage is the one place where this part of the church's vision is central. All who come to the island are pilgrims; they stand under the judgement of God's word; they need to be nourished by the word of God and by the Bread of Life; they come to repent of their sins and want to deepen their relationship with God; they have other human and spiritual needs. They come empty-handed, supplicant and perhaps not even aware of their needs. They come to walk a pilgrim path. They are part of a pilgrim people.

This sense of being a pilgrim among pilgrims finds particular expression in the night vigil and in the celebration of the sacrament of penance. When, as a priest-pilgrim, one joins the resident priests to celebrate the sacrament there is a deep sense of solidarity with the penitents who come to confession. To be there barefoot, tired and weary, and to know that we are in this together, is an experience of a kind of intimacy that I have experienced nowhere else. In this sacramental meeting, the priest is still a pilgrim among pilgrims, a sinner among sinners. He has the opportunity to minister to his fellow-pilgrims and they, through their faith, minister to him. And when he has finished 'hearing' confession, there is nothing more natural than that he kneels down and makes his own confession. Another word for equality is solidarity; it comes from an experience of being church together.

The second thing that strikes me about the Lough Derg pilgrimage is that for a few days I am precisely that, a pilgrim. For the rest of the year we define ourselves largely by our work; socially we are either alone or members of a crowd, an audience perhaps; in the economy we are seen as clients or consumers. To be addressed as a pilgrim, to be told that '250 pilgrims have come on to the island today' and to know that I was one of them – this brings out a part of who and what I am as a follower of Christ that usually does not register very strongly with me. Knowing that I am a 'pilgrim' reminds me that 'I have not here a lasting city'. It reminds me that it is more appropriate to 'travel light' than to accumulate more and more things. It helps me to face the reality that 'our true homeland is in heaven'. There is something humble and unpretentious about being a pilgrim; a pilgrim has not arrived; he/she wants to live the present moment fully; he/she lives without security but without burdens. It is an 'alternative' way of being in the world.

The third thing that strikes me about the pilgrimage is that it is very difficult. Most people in Ireland today live comfortable lives, at least in material terms. This ease or comfort is reflected in our spiritual lives. We manage most of the time to live our faith in a lifestyle that differs little from that of men and women who have no faith. The radicalism of the Sermon on the Mount impinges on us rarely. The Lough Derg pilgrimage brings home to us that the call to follow Christ is a call to a radical dying to self and a call to a life of dependence on God that only faith can sustain. Modern church teaching on the priesthood highlights the radical holiness to which the priest is called. Pope John Paul II wrote in *Pastores dabo vobis* (1992):

> For all Christians without exception, the radicalism of the gospel represents a fundamental, undeniable demand flowing from the call of Christ to follow and imitate him by virtue of the intimate communion of life with him brought about by the spirit … This same demand is made anew to priests … inasmuch as they are configured to Christ, the Head and Shepherd, equipped for and committed to the ordained ministry, and inspired by pastoral charity. (n. 27)

This radicalism finds expression in ways closely related to the evangelical counsels which Jesus proposes in the Sermon on the Mount, and among them, the intimately related counsels of obedience, chastity and poverty. A priest is called to a life of consistent prayer, faith and selflessness; he should therefore be a man possessed by the Spirit of Christ and a man deeply marked by the Paschal Mystery of the death and resurrection of Christ. To spend time 'in the desert', dislocated from the ordinary – if only for a few days – helps me to focus again on who I am as a child of God and as a minister of the gospel. It brings home to me the unbelievable mystery that Christ desires my whole heart and soul. It reminds me that in God's eyes I am indeed 'worth more than many sparrows'.

Tony Mallon

From mother to son to daughter

Lough Derg was always a tradition with my mother's family. It had a magnetic appeal.

Mystery and intrigue always surrounded my mother's and my aunt's (Maggie and Lizzy Creaney) visits to St Patrick's Purgatory. I was always quizzing them about Lough Derg, but could never comprehend its meaning. My mother often told me that until I went there, I would not understand it. She explained to me that at my tender age of ten, I was much too young to indulge in such a traumatic experience. This made me all the more determined that one day, when I was old enough, I would reach my goal and 'do' St Patrick's Purgatory.

In 1959, at the age of thirteen I acquired a job – albeit part-time – and I saved my hard-earned wages over the coming months with the intention that I would pay for my mother and myself, therefore putting her under an obligation to take me with her (even though I was under age!).

My scheming plan worked, and on a July morning I was on the St Peter's Parish trip to the infamous Lough Derg. After a six hour journey and many rosaries later (interrupted by an odd singsong), we rounded the last bend on the winding road from Pettigo. Lough Derg with Station Island planted firmly in the middle came into view. At this point a deafening, eerie silence came over the bus. The pounding of my heart seemed to be the only sound audible. I was buzzing to get off the bus and onto the island.

In expectation I watched as my mother paid for and received two metal discs and the Pilgrimage Exercise Leaflet, thus allowing us access to the boat, and moments later, the island. I realised that as a thirteen-year-old I had broken the age regulation just to fulfil my dream of many years.

I was caught up in a combined state of ecstasy, euphoria and elation. I can remember being overwhelmed by the whole occasion, but I cannot recall too many details of my initial visit. I believe that over the next three days I grew from a boy to a man, both mentally and religiously.

In August of that same year, my mother informed me that she would like to do the 'closing', if she had company. I had no hesitation in offering to go with her. The return was a lot tougher and demanding, as the first had been a bit of a novelty. But how many thirteen year olds can claim to have done the pilgrimage twice in the one season (albeit illegally, as I passed for a fifteen year old)?

Forty years on, I have continued the family tradition, not missing a single year, going twice if not three times a season. Each pilgrimage generates an increasing religious fervour that words just cannot describe.

Over all the years that I have been going to Lough Derg I have met some wonderful characters, including a blind Englishman, a hermit who walked for six days to go to Lough Derg, the famous Down footballer, Colm McAlarney, numerous Americans, Australians and Indians, but the one I remember most fondly is Hughie McGrath from Ederney who had completed the pilgrimage for at least sixty years. He had a saying which will remain etched in my memory: 'It doesn't matter how many times a man does Lough Derg, it all depends on what he does in between.' Is this not food for thought?

In 1986, due to being seriously ill with a stomach problem (only being able to take fluids, no solids for two months) I missed the 'opening' of Lough Derg. Still very ill at the time of the closing, a close friend, Peter McVeigh, who had accompanied me on numerous pilgrimages, asked me to go along with him. This I reluctantly agreed to do, going out of obligation but something within me telling me to go. Unfortunately I spent most of the three days in the First Aid area, but I was determined to stay and this I did. I felt exhausted and my health was deteriorating.

Upon returning home, on the stroke of midnight of the third day, 15 August, I asked my wife Rosetta to fry me an egg, bacon and soda farl. This she did with trepidation as the sight of food over the past two months had been making me ill. Surprisingly I ate what was put before me with no ill-effect.

I had a review appointment the next day with my doctor who, upon hearing of my midnight feast, was shocked to hear that I was now feeling much better. (This appeared to have been an impossibility due to my severe stomach problem.) Miraculously my symptoms had been alleviated and the only reason the doctor could offer was my visit to Lough Derg.

At present my religious beliefs are as strong as ever, which I attribute to my pilgrimages to Lough Derg. During my visits I usually have the privilege of leading the pilgrims for one of the 'stations' which is said in common in the basilica during the night.

I also make a special effort to help fellow-pilgrims, especially offering assistance at St Brigid's Bed as I in the past have found this one to be the most demanding and difficult of the Penitential Beds. This was particularly so for my mother who often required assistance at St Brigid's.

The tradition within my own immediate family has continued with both my daughter Jacqueline and my son Gary being regular visitors to Lough Derg.

My daughter Jacqueline asked a Protestant friend to accompany her on a pilgrimage in August 1999, with her friend knowing nothing of the Catholic faith, practices or traditions. After completing the pilgrimage, Jacqueline's friend is looking forward to 'doing' Lough Derg again. If friendship like this can be maintained by both communities and denominations on our small island, there is, no doubt, a great chance of a bright future for our religious and political differences.

Michelle Loughran

A step closer to God

'Lough Derg is an island somewhere in Donegal. It is a place where you eat nothing but dry toast, you don't wear shoes or socks and you pray a lot'.

This is not a very appealing image for a teenager with no knowledge whatsoever of what the Lough Derg pilgrimage was all about. So when my teacher proposed a trip to the island I was practically the first person to put my head down and refuse his generous offer of a few days out of school.

Lough Derg was then forgotten about until a few weeks later and the idea was brought forth again. This time to my surprise it was now my friends who were talking of going.

So, in a state of complete shock and amazement that they had even considered going, I asked dumbfoundedly 'Why?'

They laughed. Why? They said Lough Derg was a great place. It is an exciting adventure where you get to meet new people and move closer to God. This was a far cry from my perception of Lough Derg. What about the starvation, what about walking around a chapel all night with no shoes on? Did none of this matter?

Well, eventually they persuaded me to go. My excuse was that I would have been left behind by myself so I cautiously agreed to embark on their 'exciting adventure' which would make us better people! My opinion on the matter was that I would be proved right when we came back tired and weak and wondering why we had ever gone. So I left on a note of satisfaction, believing that my friends would never withstand the pressure Lough Derg had to throw at them.

On the bus journey down there was a great air of excitement

and a real sense that something good was going to happen. But that rapidly deteriorated when we arrived at the lake and, on examination of the island, the general feeling changed to, 'What have I let myself in for?' We all wanted to turn back.

But we proceeded with our journey and, after a boat ride that felt like it was going to last forever, we arrived gratefully at what felt like the 'Promised Land'.

The first thing that struck me about Lough Derg was the great calming silence. It seemed to soothe away my now disintegrating fears and I became relaxed. The atmosphere was so peaceful and this desolate island was like a totally new and different world. I instantly liked the place.

Throughout the first day I became accustomed to the pangs of hunger and it eventually came to the point where I didn't mind the not eating. It almost became natural to see people walk around in their bare feet and after a few stations I even got used to the jagged edges of the penitential beds.

The all night vigil was the hardest part and none of us had anticipated just how difficult it was going to be. But it was during this long cold night that I feel I grew closer to God and our relationship was renewed and strengthened enormously.

I began to appreciate the great comforts of the outside world that we all take for granted. I realised that without God we wouldn't be here and we should be eternally grateful for the world he has created for us.

When my time came to leave Lough Derg I felt a touch of sadness. I realised that I hadn't missed any pastimes from the modern world, like the TV or radio. But I was going to miss Lough Derg, for it had provided a secure environment that was filled with peace and it was a close-knit community for everyone who was there. At this time I considered everything in my life and this quality time alone helped me isolate the most important things and it gave me the initiative to change my life and be a better person.

When we were leaving Lough Derg and the boat pulled away from the shore, a fellow student said, 'If you look back at the island you will do the pilgrimage again'. At that moment I glanced back at the island because I knew I wouldn't be properly fulfilled until I completed St Patrick's Purgatory for the second time.

Last summer I did repeat the pilgrimage and found it to be a lot easier the second time around. I will hopefully return again in the near future, because for me each time I complete Lough Derg I take a step closer to God.

Meeting on Station Island

The annual pilgrimage from London to Lough Derg and the foundation of the London Lough Derg Committee owes its origins to a simple conversation held in the spring of 1987 after Sunday Mass on the steps of St Raphael's Parish Church, Yeading, Middlesex, between William Henry, Maurice Smith and Michael O'Shea.

We had all lived in the parish since 1969-71 and had made our lives and homes in the London borough of Hillingdon. We were all, at that time, busy with family life and immersed in our work.

On that spring day on the steps of St Raphael's, we were all discussing our forthcoming summer holidays when Maurice casually mentioned that he was thinking of 'doing the pilgrimage at Lough Derg in the summer'. Although not expecting any real response, both William and Michael immediately said they would 'love to come'.

William and Maurice had been to Lough Derg as young adults through the encouragement of their parents but it had been seventeen years since either of their last visits.

Michael's sister from Co Longford was a regular pilgrim so he had heard about the pilgrimage many times.

The following week Maurice had booked the tickets from Heathrow to Belfast and so began the first of thirteen consecutive pilgrimages together from London.

The first pilgrimage was to set the routine and format for the succeeding years and a small committee was formed with William as Chairman, Michael as Manager and Maurice as Secretary.

The first pilgrimage included members of William's family from Co Sligo; his brother and two sisters are now regular pilgrims with the London Lough Derg Committee.

The highlight of that first year was how much we all enjoyed the pilgrimage, but the success of the next twelve years is due to the encouragement from our wives, Elizabeth, Clara and Anne who alternately each year prepared the midnight dinner at the end of the pilgrimage. Sadly Clara was to die in April 1995. May God rest her soul.

During the first few years we joined the Queen's University Chaplaincy bus at their stop in Magherafelt in Co Derry. Unfortunately this was discontinued and we had to make alternative travel arrangements.

We are grateful to Maurice's sister Rosemary in Co Derry who often provided accommodation the night before and on occasions drove us to Lough Derg.

After the first five years, we decided that we would invite other members of our families and close friends both in west London and Ireland, and during the past eight years an average of 8-9 pilgrims from London together with 5-6 pilgrims from Ireland have made the journey together to Lough Derg.

To date, nearly 200 individual pilgrimages have been made from London and Ireland under the banner of the London Lough Derg Committee. Three certificates have been awarded to young persons under seventeen years who have completed the pilgrimage with us, the youngest being only fourteen.

Following the pilgrimage, the committee have held an annual dinner in October to which the pilgrims invite their spouse/ friend for a formal night out in appreciation of their support and encouragement. This event over the years has become an evening to look forward to when the Chairman welcomes our guests and toasts St Patrick's Purgatory. The committee was delighted to have Fr Pat McHugh, a member of staff at Lough Derg, as a guest at the 1998 dinner.

In April each year the committee hold their Annual General Meeting when we decide the dates to once again make the pilgrimage from London, usually in June or early July. In recent times we have hired a people carrier at Belfast Airport and the journey is completed in some luxury.

A tradition on the return journey is a visit to Clonard Monastery in west Belfast where the pilgrims pray for peace in Ireland before the afternoon flight to Heathrow.

St Patrick's Purgatory holds a very special place in the hearts of its London Committee members and we continually mention to others how much we owe in our lives to the pilgrimage at Lough Derg.

We look forward to future visits and the renewing of friendships and love of one of the most beautiful places on earth, Station Island, Lough Derg, Co Donegal.

Ann Leonard

King or pauper, everyone is equal

The month of June has a very strange effect on me, and I have no doubt, on thousands of other Lough Derg regulars. The questions: Will I go? Will I pass on it this year, if I can't get three days off during the whole summer? Will I get past 15 August before guilt gets the better of me?

The truth is, when June arrives, the thoughts of Lough Derg immediately appear and despite all my best efforts for the past fourteen years, I have not been able to really enjoy the summer, guilt-free, until I have got Lough Derg 'out of the way'. I first went to Lough Derg with my father and sister when I was sixteen years old. Throughout my father's working life he spoke of Lough Derg as his annual holiday. I have come to look on Lough Derg, not as a holiday, but as a surreal existence for two days, which is a form of escapism for me, from the real world.

The beauty of Lough Derg is that whether you are a king or a pauper, everyone is equal. Perhaps they are there for very different reasons, but they are joined in the common goal of getting through the pilgrimage as best they can. I have a number of memories of my first time on the island. As I have said, I was sixteen years old and was so confident leaving home that despite all the warnings, I never thought of bringing a coat with me.

I was only at St Brendan's Bed, walking around the outside, when my father arrived, with two long, see-through waterproof coats for my sister and I. Needless to say, a long see-through waterproof wasn't the trendiest dress code. However, very welcome and necessary on this occasion. At St Molaise's Bed, one could not see any stones, with the 'lake' that surrounded the cross in the centre.

Just about the time I was checking my sanity at approximately 3.00 am on the first night, I spied a gentleman rudely awakening many of the pilgrims with a whiff of smelling salts. I swore to my sister, in my half-conscious state, that if he came near me I would punch him in the face. At that time of night the tolerance threshold is extremely low! So much for the spirit of Lough Derg!

With the best of intentions, I sit bolt upright, not only for the 6.30 am Mass on the second day, but for all Masses. However, hell must be full of my intentions, because I can never, ever remember what the homily has been about, despite my insistence that I have stayed awake throughout.

My favourite time each day on Lough Derg is the meal time – it's not the meal that is the attraction, but the conversation that always occurs with complete strangers, around the table in the dining hall. These complete strangers are very often like long lost friends who, when they leave the island have absolutely nothing in common with each other. Lough Derg affords me an opportunity to talk to people who do not know or want to know anything about my work or my life. It allows one to converse with others, or alternatively, affords one the opportunity to be completely alone with one's thoughts, worries or thanksgivings. I always feel a great sense of relief when I get past the Sacrament of Reconciliation stage. It's not that the sacrament is that stressful or painful, but I always feel I am on the home straight, when I get over this hurdle.

Day Two is then my day to relax, pray a little, read or talk to people as I wish. I remember one year bringing a book with me, in which I became totally engrossed. That year, during the second day, the interruptions were a source of annoyance to me, including the Renewal of Baptismal Promises and the Way of the Cross. The book, which I will always remember, was an autobiography about an Irish prostitute. Not, I would imagine the most appropriate reading material for such a holy place.

Lough Derg is, if not a holy place, a peaceful place. I would not consider myself a religious person, but one is drawn to prayer and meditation and also, I believe, thanksgiving on the island. The space that Lough Derg gives me allows me the opportunity to evaluate what has taken place in my life in the past year, and also allows me to contemplate or to talk through with God, some of my hopes and wishes for the following year. I cannot say what is special about Lough Derg. I dread the thought of it for weeks before the June weekend. The facilities on the island have improved immensely since I started going to it, but the stones haven't got any smoother, and the nights haven't got any shorter.

To me, Lough Derg cannot be compared to any other pilgrimage or any other retreat that I have ever been on. There is nothing that can compare to the sense of satisfaction that one feels looking back on the island as you head for home. Twenty-four hours previous to going home, you swear never, ever again. But, while sitting in the boat, looking back at the island, one often feels – maybe it wasn't so bad!

Eugen Lang

A new rhythm of meditation

Once a year I personally need a break from my usual way of life. From time to time it is helpful to get a certain distance from work, to escape from hardship and leave my home in Switzerland and my dear family behind. For that reason I regularly come to the west of Ireland for long walks to lonely lakes and hills. It is through my studies of Irish history and folklore that I became acquainted with St Patrick's and St Colmcille's spiritual heritage and their highly developed monastic and artistic culture.

It is by pure chance that I discovered the Lough Derg pilgrimage fourteen years ago. Although I have come back as pilgrim many times, each time I am still deeply impressed by the helpful exercises which reflect a wise tradition from early Christianity. The programme leaves me enough time to search the truth and to meditate on the sense of life. I am discovering a lot of new feelings, as the following few examples show: my start at the first station is usually not so easy, because when kneeling down on the hard naked stones around St Patrick's Cross, I feel that I am coming down on a rock of truth and on a ground of modesty. On my way walking around the basilica I always switch off from the fast pace of business; by marching with the rosary I come to a new rhythm of meditation. Praying side by side with Irish people old and young, I feel a deep unity through faith and heart.

This gives me a view of the universality of the church as well as the relationship between its individual people. Last year when I came to the circling of the basilica late in the afternoon, I stopped, overlooking the lake from the terrace, watching the golden sun in its evening brightness which was slowly approaching the far hills. I admired the suns rays reflected on the water by thousands of little sparkling waves; the splendour of it was blown to our shore by a mild westerly wind. This carpet of light and wisdom is leading me to new horizons of our loving God. I will gratefully come again to this place, for penance, prayer and reconciliation, because here I have found an island of discovering and recovering.

Simon Kennedy

Lough Derg

A basilica drapes the Island like a hood.
Barefoot pilgrim meander
Over your hobble stones
Of penitential beds.
St Patrick – Pray for us.
St Brigid – pray for us.
St Columba – Pray for us.
Black tea and toast
Black toast and tea
Sinner save your soul
Toss and turn toward the sea.
Fumble into the dark night
Weary vigil keep
St Brendan – Pray for us.
St Molaise – Pray for us.
European bishop and potentate
Did penance here.
St Patrick saw demons in a cave –
Shown to him by God
The afters of the cravings of a guilty hooded mind.
Where pay-as-you-earn taxpayers
Heal their ailing lives
Wincing out the nicotine
In the embrocation of a well bruised sole,
Son of man – Have mercy on me.
The Stationbeds leave bunions and corns in fligits.
The monotonous silence transcends.
The mist falls with real dark grime.
Retreat begins within
'I believe'.

Louise Kelly

True community, shared purpose

The 'Lough Derg Experience' began for me as an innocent four-teen-year-old during the 1991 pilgrimage season. I embarked on the island with minimal knowledge of what the pilgrimage involved, except for the few fragments of information that I had managed to pick up from parents, relations and neighbours who had been there previously. None of those 'saved souls' were too forthcoming with information – they told me just what I needed to know, in case that the true story might discourage me. I realise in hindsight that this tactic was indeed very deliberate and very necessary. Needless to say I survived the rigours of the pilgrimage – youth was on my side as well as ignorance!

Putting the painful memories aside, my most vivid and inspiring memory of the place was the way in which music was treated within the liturgies. At that time I was becoming increasingly involved with church music in my own parish, but in all honesty, I had never experienced anything like the liturgy on Lough Derg before – a congregation of seven hundred people, all of whom had not sung together ever before, were singing their hearts out! A young clerical student by the name of John, who undertook the role of cantor with such ease, led us in song assisted by Leonard Dorrian from Killybegs, a young organ scholar at that time in St Patrick's College, Maynooth. Together they managed to bring the pilgrimage to life for all of us. In a very practical way, through the medium of music, they managed to give us, a group of strangers meeting for the first time that day, a true sense of community with a shared sense of purpose.

That experience is one that I have carried with me through

the years and in particular have tried to sustain and develop throughout the six seasons that I worked on Lough Derg in the roles of both cantor and organist. Throughout those six pilgrimage seasons (1993–1998) that I spent as part of the team on Lough Derg, I had the good fortune to work with many people who shared a similar enthusiasm for music in the liturgy. Each of us came from different backgrounds and different dioceses, which resulted in broadening the potential of the whole liturgical experience, and in particular, the potential of the music.

My professional experience on Lough Derg has opened my eyes and mind to the potential for congregational singing within any community; in particular within the Irish Catholic community, who are renowned for their unwillingness to participate in such activities. There is no shortage of talent and ability, but rather of the sense of community and shared purpose that only seem to manifest themselves within the context of the pilgrimage to Lough Derg.

Colm Hogan

A lesson in humility

The first time I visited Lough Derg was in 1989. It was as a pilgrim and I had managed to persuade three of my friends to come with me. We went up to the island by bus. One of my friends Pat, had bought Mars bars and apples that morning to bring with him. Obviously he had not believed me about the fasting for three days! However, as we made our journey onwards towards Donegal, whilst talking to other pilgrims, it slowly began to dawn on Pat that I was telling the truth!

The first time as a pilgrim was almost a novel one. Stories of walking barefoot around beds of stone, eating only toast and drinking black tea once a day, all while keeping vigil for a whole twenty four hours with no sleep, sounded quite unbelievable, but reality hit as soon as we set foot on the island and our first sight was bare feet everywhere.

We survived our first pilgrimage despite Pat buying a huge cream cake on the way home in Sligo. He didn't eat it, just bought it to tease and tempt everyone on the bus. Not surprisingly, Pat has never returned to Lough Derg!

I returned the following year with my mother. She had been to Lough Derg three times in the early 1950s but had not returned since then. It was almost as if my first pilgrimage had tempted her to go again. My family of course blamed me for my mother going and I was threatened that if she came back unwell, it was all my fault. However, she sailed through it, even if she used smelling salts to keep her awake at times. Second time around was, to be honest, a tough struggle. There was no sense of novelty this time for me but the company of my mother and neighbours Peggy and Geraldine kept me going, and awake! I remember dozing off at morning Mass and the next thing I woke up, got a fright and began saying the Our Father out loud in the middle of Mass. Maybe my struggle this time around reflected the struggle within myself at the time. It certainly gave the others a laugh!

I always look back on that particular pilgrimage as a major influence in my decision to go towards priesthood.

My third pilgrimage was a few years later; again I managed to persuade a friend to come along. Jack also has returned since and my only abiding memory of this pilgrimage was now that I had completed the pilgrimage three times I would never have to go to Lough Derg again!

However, I did return in the summer of 1997, not as a pilgrim but as a deacon to work on the island for three weeks. I had shoes on, the best food I had ever tasted and sleep every night. I really enjoyed the stay, meeting the pilgrims, telling them how much I ate for dinner or supper, but most of all it was a real privilege to meet people where they were at, in their struggles and joys of life. A great privilege to pray with these people.

During my three weeks a few 'famous' people came to the island: Daniel O'Donnell, Johnny Logan, Celia Larkin, Greg Blaney: a testament to the fact that Lough Derg appeals to everyone.

Lough Derg confers equality on its pilgrims in a unique way. Once the shoes are taken off there are no ranks or classes. Everyone is in it together, helping each other out, praying with each other. My stay on the island as one looking on gave me great hope for my own faith and acts as a great witness of pilgrimage and reconciliation to my priesthood today.

One week before my ordination in June 1998 I returned to Lough Derg for my fourth time as a pilgrim. Something drew me back to the island as something mysterious had drawn me the other times, but I was delighted to have the opportunity to go back in the days before taking my first steps of priesthood. It gave me the opportunity to reflect and prepare for my ordination day. It also gave me space and a chance to go back to the place which was a turning point on my journey into priesthood.

I finish with a story that I told pilgrims in my first homily on Lough Derg:

When I returned home from my first pilgrimage I waited up until midnight to eat some food: chips and two battered sausages from the local chipper. Launching into my celebration supper, my brother Hubert walked in and asked for, or rather demanded, one of my sausages. Needless to say I was not in the mood for sharing, having fasted for three days. So he said to me, 'So much for you going to Lough Derg if you can't share your food when you come home.' I was still learning the true meaning of Lough Derg in my home in Tipperary. The true meaning for me is *sharing*. By the way, I gave my brother one of my sausages! A Lough Derg lesson in humility learnt far beyond its shores!

Vincent Henriot

Discovery

For many years my love of Ireland has driven me to explore in minute detail its incredible beauty. It was thus, on a fine end of an Autumn evening, that I found myself by sheer chance in front of the entrance to St Patrick's Purgatory. Everything was silent. I did not dare proceed any further and I moved away intrigued by what I had sensed from this small island, nestling in the middle of a great lake.

The replies to questions that I asked to try to gain further information were hardly reassuring. What had been described to me as a place of pilgrimage was often referred to as a place of suffering. I was however tempted …

Two years ago, the first anniversary of the death of my son and the accompanying pain left me in such a state of disarray that I decided to go and pray on this little isle in the middle of a lake.

Recently, a friend who is aware that I did the pilgrimage for the past two years asked me, rather sceptically I felt, what good it had done me. Without any hesitation I replied, 'Twice, I have come closer to our God.' This reply came from the heart. The memory lives with me and fortifies me. I am grateful to God for having taken me by the hand and led me closer to him.

Nor do I forget the additional gifts of getting acquainted with the priests who work on the island and sharing so much with other pilgrims.

As long as there is strength left in my body, I will travel every year from France to Lough Derg. There I will take the little boat which carries the pilgrims to the basilica and penitential beds and start a new pilgrimage.

Vincent Henriot

That pilgrim was right

Tonight, as mist does,
emotion has filtered through to me.
Why is that so?

I think it is because that short day
on the isle
has been like passing by a slightly opened door.
You were,
my God,
somewhere behind that door.
I didn't see anything
but I felt the blow of your love.
Do you know it's a lot?

In my bare feet,
just able to pray with my body,
I have been, those few days, one of your sheep.
You were,
my God,
the star that showed us the way.
You had entrusted the protection of your flock
to the priests of Lough Derg.
We felt loved and protected
by You
by them.

A pilgrim told me:
'You are not here without any reason'
My God,
to make me understand,
you chose,
that extremely beautiful nature,
that so simple and true human warmth,
that faith in you so shared,
that prayer so powerful and constant.

How deeply you love me!
And how strongly you expect my love!

That pilgrim was right!

Judith Handschin

Extract from pilgrim's diary 1993

17 July, Saturday

I have an appointment with Benedicte for a walk. Before, I go to hire a bike for Sunday. Benedicte asks me how I feel. Immediately I start to cry. 'I feel horrible, I don't know what I am doing here. That's not what I want: to hire a bike to see the landscape. I want more, there must be something more.' And I don't know, what could be more … After a while Benedicte asks: 'Do you want to go to a monastery?' My eyes become big. Never, ever had I thought about something like this; the question touches me very deep. 'Yes of course, that's what I want – how do you know?' She takes me to the priests in Donegal Town. The one who is there is astonished. It never happened that someone came with this question. In a big book he looks to find something. The older priest comes. 'But what are you looking for in the book? We have the most beautiful place in the world just around the corner: it's Lough Derg.' I hear Lough Derg and I know this is the place. (I never had heard of Lough Derg before as I live in Switzerland and am not a Catholic.) The younger priest says: 'But this is very Catholic.' 'Ja-ja.' 'And you have to walk barefooted.' 'Ja-ja.' 'And one has to fast. Only water and bread.' 'Ja-ja.' 'And you may not sleep a whole night.' 'Ja-ja.'

I ring. Of course everyone is allowed to go. I cancel the bike for the next day. When my doubts come Benedicte says, 'It is ok, I know it.'

18 July 1993, Sunday

I arrive in Lough Derg and I know this is what I was looking for. *I am at home.*

A letter to Fr Mohan, a few days later:

Dear Fr Mohan

Firstly I want to say the whole atmosphere of Lough Derg and everybody there is so open and friendly. I really felt very safe.

Second I want to share my feelings and my thoughts about Lough Derg: Somebody said to me: 'Lough Derg is very Catholic.' For me it is more than Catholic, older than Catholic. And I wonder if the prayers have always been the ones you pray now. I could imagine that in the older times people prayed for the earth and the weather too. And the stations outside are praying with the earth and especially if it is raining, with the water too and I think with the whole body.

I think the movement is very important, this going three times around the outside and inside. I could imagine that it would be more harmonious if one could change the direction from inside out again (but I can see with so many people it is not possible), so that it is like breathing in and breathing out and you would have the connection to nature on the earth again, with the seasons.

Then there are nine points in one station where you kneel. There are actually ten but at St Patrick's Cross you kneel twice and that is special again because ten is a number of a new beginning and nine stations to do. Nine is the number of completion – the number of God. Three days you fast and three times three is nine again.

You do three stations before the vigil. Three is the number of spirituality of the Trinity – Father, Son and Holy Spirit. You prepare yourself spiritually for the vigil. At night you do four stations: four is the number of nature, a physical number (four seasons, four directions – east, west, etc – four apostles). You connect what you have prepared during the day with your body even more because it is at night and you don't sleep.

And then you get the sacrament of reconciliation after seven stations – a purification before you go to the eighth station (again a holy number). At last the consciousness to Christ with the Way of the Cross before the completion with the ninth station.

Ragheed Ganni

From Nineveh to Lough Derg

The flow of our lives, like that of the course and journey of a fast moving river, carries us along, brings us through the various twists and turns of experience, planned and unplanned, through times of the quick white water, of deep broad calm meanders and times spent in the eddies and in the shallows until we are deposited like fine silt along the riverbed of the places we find ourselves and the people with whom we come into contact. It was rather by accident than design that I found myself in Lough Derg the first time. The flow of life had carried me from the banks of the mighty Tigris in Iraq, to the Tiber in Rome where I study, and flowed into a remote lough and its island in Co Donegal, St Patrick's Purgatory.

I remember clearly my first day on Lough Derg, asking such questions: 'What am I doing here? Am I mad? What are these people doing here? What sort of place is this exactly?' The wind, the rain, the cold, the weather! I remember thinking 'What a place is this, yet here I am and here I must stay. I will overcome all of this and help the staff to organise the various activities around the island.' Through the days and weeks I began to learn about the place, discovering its own particular style and history. Slowly those first impressions, a mixture of curiosity and horror, gave way to a deeper appreciation of both the rich heritage of Celtic Spirituality of the island and of the island experience, and the reasons why people came and came back to the island. Though while the programme of the Purgatory entails very public and physically demanding penances, punishing in many respects, the exercises both around the beds and night liturgy of the basilica is followed by all pilgrims in a conscientious and prayerful manner. I was really impressed by the devotion of the pilgrims, so much so that at the end of my work on Lough Derg I decided to go on pilgrimage myself.

During my two summers in St Patrick's Purgatory, I have met a lot of people and each had his or her own reasons for being on Lough Derg – in thanksgiving, for a sick relation or friend, children doing exams or awaiting results, out of habit, out of curiosity, yet above all from a deep faith to join the suffering of their sore feet, and empty stomachs and tiredness, with suffering all over the world; the homeless and the hungry and leaving behind them the cares and concerns of the material life for a few days and barefooted, stand equal to their brothers and sisters.

The next year I decided to return to work on Lough Derg I was given a job again, for five weeks this time. Now that I had experienced life on St Patrick's Purgatory, I was looking forward to returning to the beautiful liturgies celebrated on the Island. The liturgical action, both inside and outside the basilica evoked in me the close presence of God, his love and mercy for us all.

Lough Derg is quite unique. A place where you go with heavy burdens, leaving them there touched by the hand of God; pilgrims stand barefooted as children of the one God. God, his grace which brings that inner peace which we all seek and which above all makes us an apostle, a disciple of Christ. As Monsignor Richard Mohan, the Prior of Lough Derg, said in one of his homilies: 'As Jesus crossed the lake to the other side to bring the news of the kingdom, thus the pilgrims of Lough Derg, after finishing their pilgrimage, cross the lake to the other side to bring the news of the kingdom. They bring healing and good news to their families and friends.'

On the third day, after fulfilling the demands of the island, pilgrims put on their shoes and walk to the boat, and on to Pettigo and beyond. There is an old saying that runs to the effect that those who look back to the island will return there. True or not, St Patrick's Purgatory, Lough Derg, is less 'somewhere' one has 'gone' and more 'somewhere' that is carried about in our present, in our thoughts and lives. And yet, those who keep their eyes fixed on the mainland on the small pier ahead do return too.

On the Island of Lough Derg I sat watching the water being gently lifted by the wind lapping against the shore and remembered the words of the Psalmist: 'By the rivers of Babylon, there we sat down and wept when we remembered Sion.' I have travelled from my home by the banks of the rivers of Babylon, to a place I thought was the end of the world and to an island on a remote lake in Co Donegal. There, 'at the end of the world' I have sat down and been with the pilgrims 'doing the beds', being annoyed by feasting midges I have sat – though not wept – and remembered not Sion but my home of Nineveh and above all the great thing that binds these two places together, namely the Christian faith.

La Flynn

Not too sacred to be written

It was in 1978 that I first worked on Lough Derg, as a priest. My first days were a baptism of water and fire: the Friday and Saturday of a Bank Holiday weekend with 500-and-something pilgrims arriving on the Friday and 1009 (the figure remains firmly etched in my memory!) on the Saturday. Prior Flood was at the helm and I was very much the new boy, sent at short notice by Bishop Mulligan to help out for ten days until Liam MacDaid would finish a course he was then following.

The Friday was quite mesmerising as it was a matter of getting things up-and-running, and although I had made the *turas* several times I was a total novice to the behind-the-scenes mechanics of the pilgrimage. It boiled down to tagging along after Richard Mohan and following directions as best I could. To be honest I was more than a little in awe of the honour, as I saw it, of being chosen on such a prestigious team as the 'Lough Derg priests' – even if only as a sub! But when Saturday brought its compliment of pilgrims, all 1009 of them, and wet conditions into the bargain, the awesome turned to awful. I knew nothing of the logistics of packing them all into the basilica (later I would appreciate more clearly how pilgrims swell when they are wet), of 'inside stations' to make it possible to get the required three done on the first day, of the knock-on effects in the dining rooms of such crowds, and I knew nothing certainly of the many and nefarious wiles and ruses that pilgrims might and did come up with to 'solve' the problems for themselves! The Sunday morning and early afternoon in a confessional in St Mary's was the easiest bit of it all; at least I had some idea of what I should be doing in a confession box …

I had two further short stretches on the island that 1978 season: a week in mid-July and the August fortnight. Another memory returns. As we gathered the pilgrims for Mass one evening, I noticed a man of about my own age moving into St Mary's. Helpful as ever, I followed him to let him know that Mass would in fact be in the basilica. He told me he was not going to Mass, and could not be persuaded otherwise. Flummoxed but dutiful, I sought experienced counsel from Fr Mohan, who pointed me in the direction of the staff house where Prior Flood was just then emerging to make his way up towards the basilica. When I told the Prior of my case he simply said, 'Follow me, young man', and I trotted after him into St Mary's. The exchange with my deviant friend was not unkind, but short and very much to the point. 'Are you a pilgrim?' The bare-footed one could only answer, 'Yes, I'm a pilgrim.' 'The pilgrims,' said Prior Flood, 'are in the basilica.' And he stood back with his hand extended in the direction of the door of St Mary's. I don't know if it was his unassailable logic that made the difference where earlier my gentle reasoning had failed, but without any to-do the pilgrim joined his fellow-pilgrims in the basilica. And I had had a lesson on one style of church leadership.

So many stories could be told or re-told. Over the fourteen seasons that I worked on Lough Derg, 1978-1991, there were many opportunities for telling my stories and hearing the stories of others. I won't swear to it that the tales passed unchanged from one telling to another, but that's how stories are. The last night of the season, 14 August each year, had its own late-night 'liturgy of the word'. The memorable events of the season would be rehearsed and the calls to 'tell about the time that...' would go around, invoking memories which became ours only by proxy, as we told again the tales we had heard others tell.

There is another stratum of Lough Derg gospel which will never be printed in a book. Much of it is too sacred to be written, perhaps even to be retold. Some of it has been whispered in a confessional context, more has been explored in a chat somewhere about the island, often without even the formality of such a title as counselling. I think of the wee woman who finally ended her endless confession with the line, 'Thank God – and thank you, Father', repeated over and over. I think of so many people whom I met, some of them once, others again and again, on Lough Derg. I think of Lough Derg friendships which have enriched my life; I give thanks for so many opportunities of personal growth for myself and pastoral service to others. I take particular delight in the development I have witnessed of a rich and vibrant liturgical style in the worthy setting of the basilica, at once simple and dignified and deeply participative. I rejoice in the vision of those whom I have known, both pilgrims and staff members, who have believed in the Lough Derg pilgrimage, have valued their own experience of it and have sought in different ways to share it with others. According to the legend, God gave the Purgatory of Lough Derg to St Patrick. To ensure that it will continue in a living and life-giving way into the new millennium is a sacred trust to our generation, under the grace of God. May the One who began this good work among us bring it to fulfilment.

Stale Dyrvik

Through Norwegian eyes

My first glimpse of St Patrick's Purgatory, one day in early May 1988: Standing on the deserted shore, under a leaden sky, I stared at the mirage in the middle of the lake. I knew I had to come back.

July 1989: I am a pilgrim for the first time! The heatwave over Ireland offers excellent conditions for starting to learn the prayers and the exercises. Fasting and staying awake is tackled quite well. But the myriads of nightly midges would have driven me mad, had it not been for the hood of my jacket.

1990-1996: Seven consecutive pilgrimages under 'normal' conditions: wind, a lot of rain and bitter cold. Fasting never bothered me. But it was impossible to avoid the cold, creeping up into my body through the bare feet. Every time, the late night of the vigil felt like a trip to the vicinities of death. During the last station on the last morning, the pain of my feet and my body inevitably turned into a sacrifice over which I no longer had control.

But why not mention the good moments? The beautiful liturgies in the basilica, and the positive spiritual guidance of the priests. The numerous personal encounters and conversations that brought me into contact with so many extraordinary people. And not to forget the heavenly feeling of putting on socks and shoes on the day of departure.

But what have I come to consider the essence of the pilgrimage? From the very beginning 1500 years ago, it was a matter of confession and penance. Each pilgrim struggling in his/her own world of sin and grace. The sacrament of reconciliation still is the heart of the matter. But to me, penance took surprising directions. I soon felt that the right thing to do was to pray for others and to offer my insignificant sacrifices to alleviate their burdens. I don't think that prayers and hidden sacrifices should be preferred to direct words and deeds of support and consolation, but it is wonderful to be part of a community where both visible and invisible love is flowing and making miracles.

Prayer and sacrifice for fellow humans, that is one fundamental part of the pilgrimage. The other part may appear more selfish. The whole practical arrangement of the pilgrimage is a peculiar historical example of how the church has taught self-control and self-discipline to its members. I know that all my self-inflicted pain will contribute nothing to make me worthy of God's forgiveness, but the ability to master mental and bodily strain by means of will and determination is part of being a free, independent and responsible person. And the mystery of human and divine love is based upon that freedom, so don't underestimate what I am talking about. As a former Lutheran, I was taught to think of Protestants as strong individuals and Catholics as passive crowd members. That interpretation was not confirmed in the real world: I have never felt the uniqueness and the value of my person so strongly – and humbly – as during my stays in St Patrick's Purgatory.

The Lough Derg Pilgrimage is one of the finest jewels of the Christian world. Only an exceptional people can create and maintain such a spiritual institution. I thank the Irish for letting me so generously into their treasury. The experience has changed me forever.

Pauline Duffy

Labour and love

I first went to work on Lough Derg as a cleaner in July 1996 when I was sixteen. On my arrival I was horrified at the complete isolation that stood before me. The island was worse than I imagined it to be. It felt unbelievably small and I was shocked that there wasn't even a tuck shop for staff. I was brought up to my bedroom which I was to share with a girl called Sharon from Monaghan, who I had never met before. The other cleaner was Liz Duffy who I knew to see around home but had never actually been talking to. I suppose the fact that I didn't know any of the other staff just added to my misery. The cleaner's uniform was an unfashionable light blue and navy pinafore; fortunately it wasn't long until the Prior decided to abandon it!

For the first week I hated the place. Every day seemed to drag and I remember ringing home telling everybody I was having a great time but at the same time crying quietly on the other end of the phone. On our day off we could either go home or stay on the island. On my my first day off, I decided to stay because I knew that if I went home I would never come back!

The work wasn't difficult. We had to clean the toilets, sweep and wash floors and generally keep the island in a clean condition. We didn't have to meet any deadlines like some of the other staff. There was one thing I didn't like about the job and that was cleaning up after a pilgrim who had been sick.

By the last week I had come to love the place. I had made some great friends and although we were supposed to go to bed at 11.00 pm, five of us would sit up talking, drinking Coca-Cola and eating kit-kats which someone had brought in from Pettigo, until the early hours of the morning. On the fifteenth of August we were to leave. The last two weeks had been great crack and Liz and I decided to go back the following year.

I returned in 1997 and 1998 to work in the staff kitchen. This involved helping prepare the food and general housekeeping duties. The staff house is always really busy so there was always plenty of work to be done. Still bedtime was at 11.00 pm which I thought was too early. Anyhow I sat up late one night watching television with a few others and we fell asleep in the staff TV room. One of us didn't get up in time the next morning and we were called to account for ourselves. After that I could see why there was a bedtime rule but I can't really say I started to pay much attention to it!

Last year I spent most of the summer on Lough Derg, working in the staff kitchen again. Peggy is the cook, but each week, on Thursday, on her day off, I took over and cooked for 35-40 staff. I have to say I learned so much about catering for numbers last year! I had never made a scone or cooked a chicken in my life until I had to do it for the first time one Thursday last summer. I also had the opportunity of working with the basilica staff. I helped with the confessional queues and was cantor at Mass occasionally, which I really enjoyed. Last year for the first time staff outings to other islands on the lake and walks around the mainland shores to other holy sites were organised. These helped bring staff together in a relaxed and fun atmosphere and proved to be very worthwhile.

As a member of staff, I think Lough Derg is the type of place you will either love or hate. For me it is a place I love and I will go back. Although I did not stay in contact with everybody I worked with during the last four years, I did make some very good friends that I don't think I will ever forget.

Clare Dowling

Not gentle but grace-filled

In the summer of 1997 I was among the first group of young lay people to have the privilege of working on Lough Derg in a pastoral capacity. I was studying theology and philosophy at All Hallows College in Dublin at the time, when I came across an advertisement for pastoral workers on a college noticeboard. I have to admit to being highly amused by the looming title of 'St Patrick's Purgatory' as the main heading and by the provision of 'room and board' as part of the salary. This did not seem to be much of an incentive. Nevertheless I was drawn to the notice several times before deciding to apply for the job. Part of me thought I had a cheek to apply at all because I had not yet any formal qualification in theology and I have never been at the forefront of voluntary parish work. I was also acutely aware of my own faith struggle and felt unworthy and nervous of pre-senting myself as a convinced Christian which is what I thought one ought to be on Lough Derg. I decided though that nothing too disastrous could happen to me in the space of three and a half weeks which was the term of the job, so off I went to Donegal.

The island is an inhibiting place when you first see it from across the lake. I had never been there before, nor had I seen a picture of it, so I was stunned to see such substantial buildings pressed onto this tiny piece of land. It looked like the remnants of a city submerged after a flood. Chugging across the water on that first day I felt sick with apprehension. Little did I know then just how much Lough Derg would profoundly affect my life.

I became involved in a strict, smooth-running system of ritual and liturgy. The days are clearly laid out and by and large do not change. The work was intensive and demanding although my job description gave much room for the evolution of this new position. I was part of a team of people which included lay, cleric, religious and seminarians whose first and last priority was the pilgrims. We served at morning and evening Mass. We were Ministers of the Eucharist. We read at the Stations of the Cross and at Night Prayer. We walked around the island during the day just talking to and being available to the pilgrims. We were there in some way to ensure that an ancient tradition continued and in another equally important way to both respond and witness to the mixed bag of humanity that walks barefoot on cold stone for two and a half days at a time. I believe that Monsignor Mohan's motivation in bringing lay pastoral workers to the island was to present a more accurate reflection of the changing face of the church today. This is a noble gesture in a place which could attempt to be the last bastion of clericalism in Ireland.

The unique aspect of my job was in the foundation of a discussion group, primarily for second day pilgrims who have a lot of time for reflection. I would put up a notice in the morning stating the time and place of the gathering and then I would wait to see who showed up. Numbers ranged from three to nearly fifty on one particularly scary day. The groups were a source of fascination to me. I was struck by the sheer ordinariness of the pilgrims and moved by their willingness to share their own faith struggles with the rest of us. I suppose we expect people who go on pilgrimage to be a bit pious, to have somehow arrived at a conclusion about God and faith. What I learned, especially through those groups, was what probably should have been obvious from the start: that the pilgrimage is a most profound symbol of the faith journey which is in turn life's journey. If you arrive feeling certain of your image of God then there was little point in making the trip. Relationship with God is dynamic and mysterious and cannot hope for full intimacy before death. I did not have to hide my uncertainty from these people.

During my stay I decided to take off my shoes and become a pilgrim myself. Lough Derg is a different experience without food and sleep. I went from enjoying the time to reflect alone on the first day to feeling exhausted during the vigil throughout that night. That was the most difficult time on Lough Derg for me. It was a liminal or a threshold experience. I was tired, cold, hungry and unexpectedly sad. Of course we all feel a bit miserable when we notice the lack of a meal and a warm bed (as rare as this is for the majority of us), but this sadness also had something to do with praying and not knowing who or what I was praying to or why. That night I felt stripped bare and I had to ask myself that most fundamental of questions: 'Who am I?' The answer pertained to both where I came from and where I was going; in other words, my journey. I received no easy answer then or since, but I have come to understand that experience as grace-filled. The spirit of Lough Derg is not a gentle one, but it is the same spirit which accompanies us all and teaches us to live with our questions.

By mutual agreement, my stay on the island was extended to nine and a half weeks in total. I loved the place. Chugging across the water on that last day I felt a mixture of sadness that an invaluable period in my life had ended and gratitude that I had been given such a gift.

Agnes Mary Devine

The barriers are down

It must be up to half a century ago or more since I first heard of Lough Derg. A friend of my mother's called for a cup of tea one day and she told me afterwards that he (Alec McSorley, RIP), had come out of Lough Derg for the fortieth time a few days previous. I gathered it was a place of prayer and penance and if you did it three times you were sure of heaven! Alec walked across the hills barefooted and fasting to placate the God he believed in. He was from the parish of Termonamongan (Aghyaran) and was a gentleman of intelligence and integrity.

I was fourteen when I went for the first time with my twenty-year-old farming cousin. We cycled along the old cart roads of the same parish and were lashed by the various intermittent showers. I was proud to be up to it with my manly cousin. Lough Derg in those days had its basilica, confessions chapel, priests' house and a row of two storeyed houses for the men and women pilgrims. These scantily furnished houses had their open fires and huge black kettles of water on the ready for the black tea. The housekeepers were never without a job between drying out the wet clothing of new arrivals, making oatmeal cakes, toasting endless loaves of bread and making 'soup'. Oh boy, what rich soup that was! When my cousin directed me to the kitchen for soup after the first station I was thrilled. I hadn't been told that soup was on the menu. What a land I got when I was handed a cup of boiling water with a dusting of pepper on the top. But, the imagination was satisfied if not the stomach and off you went to complete your 'stations'.

The Prior in those days was strict and was there to ensure that you gained all the indulgences and graces awarded for two days of prayer and penance. I say that in all honesty and without criticism because the rule was that you did without sleep for twenty-four hours and if you happened to nod off within that time you could forfeit your plenary indulgence.

The first-timer to the island is never prepared for what she finds there. Up to a thousand people are moving around the stony pathways, barefooted and with layers of clothing and rainproofs on them. You get the impression that all the poor and downtrodden are gathered together to do penance. The barriers are down. The wind and rain have washed off the ladies' make-up and undone their latest hairdo. Empty stomach and lack of sleep have wreaked havoc on the rosy-cheeked good lookers. But when the newcomer mingles with the crowds and gets into conversation with the strangers around her, she realises that the mix of rich and poor, professional and lay, old and young, is impressive. Someone will point out so-and-so from the faculty of law at Queen's University or the lead soprano in *Madame Butterfly* at the Gaeity or the big coloured man who is a bishop in a faraway African diocese, etc, etc. So, your horizons widen considerably and your sense of pride in belonging to the Catholic Church swells.

Those who 'did' Lough Derg in the early days believed in a God of mercy, generosity and forgiveness. They had many favours to thank God for and many more to ask. They needed to make up to their God for their shortcomings and make a fresh start. Fewer people may be going to the island now but their faith hasn't diminished. After an absence of twenty years I went back there last year and was struck by the deep fervour and spirituality of the pilgrims. There was no sense of haste to get the stations completed and there were no short cuts taken over the 'Beds'. The spirit of prayerfulness was remarkable and the air of quiet, tangible. The number of young people taking and given leadership roles in pastoral work there was most gratifying; accomplished organists and cantors replacing one another; others leading a discussion group; ushers of confession queues, etc. The quality of liturgies and para-liturgies by ordained and lay ministers was inspiring and challenging. On reflection, it was reassuring that a spirituality and dedication of such quality was full of promise for the future.

So, well done to the pastors of the Clogher diocese for keeping the season of pilgrimage open to the faithful at no little cost. It augurs well for the twenty-first century and I feel that a New Visitation will come to our shores and the present day accommodation on the island will not be sufficient to provide for the flow of pilgrims.

Paul Corrigan

Improved but never changed

I have made the Lough Derg pilgrimage about a dozen times in my lifetime and, although the first occasion was away back in 1950, I still have vivid memories of the experience. Even though I was well advised by my elders as to the difficulties and discomforts I would encounter, I found the reality to be very much different to what I had expected. I know that I was quite excited when I arrived at the 'shore' and was eagerly looking forward to the boat trip across to the island. I took my place in the queue which had formed on the pier and eventually I embarked on the St Patrick which was the largest of the three boats, all of which were oared by a number of men. It took about a half-hour to make the crossing.

Arriving on the island I went to the hospice and removed my shoes and socks before beginning the spiritual exercises. Before beginning the 'beds', I had to take my place in the queue and it was then that I had my first experience of Lough Derg midges. It was a dull, clammy day and these creatures were in billions and I was 'eaten alive'. Strangely enough, in all my subsequent visits I have never encountered such an attack as on that first occasion. I wonder would it be that nowadays the Prior takes advantage of modern technology and has those trees sprayed?

By the time we had started our vigil, the weather had become very unpleasant and it was raining heavily. As the night wore on I was very cold and got very sick. It was so cold that I thought the midges were a less extreme punishment than the weather. At this time I was having serious regrets for having come to the island at all and was forming resolutions never to return.

Determined not to sleep during the night, I was relieved to

have completed the indoor stations. Mass was a particularly difficult time to stay awake. After Mass the opportunity to wash and change was very welcome. The advice of experienced pilgrims that you had the battle won when you have the night over was heartening. However, it still seemed an awful long time until the end of the vigil at 10.00 pm. The second day was very pleasant with a nice warm breeze and not a sign of a midge. I wandered around the island at will, meeting and talking to other pilgrims. Meeting Jimmy Murray, the legendary Roscommon footballer, who captained his county to two All-Ireland victories in 1943 and 1944, was a special treat for me, a young Fermanagh football enthusiast, and well worth the inconvenience of a Lough Derg pilgrimage.

With such a pleasant day and exalted company, time passed quickly and soon it was time for evening Mass. Afterwards it was back to the 'hotel' for more black tea and dry toast and now it was only the matter of an hour or so until bedtime. When the vigil candle was extinguished I can recall how glad I was to have reached this point and to be heading for bed. Sleep came quickly and after a restful night, suddenly it was 5.45 am and rising time again. The hospice was now buzzing with activity, with everyone rushing around getting ready for Mass. After Mass I completed my last station outside. Then it was back to the hospice to get on my socks and shoes and take my place on the pier to await the boat's departure.

When I reached the mainland again the first thing I did was to buy a bottle of lemonade from one of the many roadside vendors who had stalls there in those days. I think that lemonade was the best I have ever tasted. Within an hour I was back home – pleased with myself but feeling very tired.

Down the years the rules and regulations governing the Lough Derg pilgrimage have remained unchanged. But there are many other welcome changes which have taken place. Many fine new buildings have been erected and others renovated. Heating has been installed in the basilica, the hospices and the rest rooms. These improvements mean an awful lot to pilgrims.

Coffee is now available as well as tea for those who prefer it and there is both brown and white toast. Another very noticeable change is the dress attire. In the 1950s women were never seen in trousers – the nuns are even wearing them now! Men also had to be careful. I recall that on my first visit when making my way towards the basilica for some of the devotions, I was carrying my coat on my arm when I was approached by one of the priests who warned me to be sure to put on my coat before I entered the church. The change in people's smoking, or is it non-smoking, habits is very marked on Lough Derg. At one time everyone seemed to smoke. Indeed the 'fags' were a great friend especially between the stations at night and during that long second day. The falling off in numbers doing the pilgrimage is another feature of modern times. Gone are the days when several hundred would come on to the island each day. Now it is but a fraction. Speaking from my own selfish viewpoint – now that my joints are cringing and squeaking a little more each year – I don't think I could make it around the beds with the numbers that were there fifty years ago.

I must say that, in a strange sort of way, I have enjoyed each and every one of my visits to Lough Derg. I have many lovely memories and experiences and I hope to be able to return to the island a few more times at least. Perhaps my most abiding memory is that of leaving the island: you are there on the pier mingling with people, many of whom you got to know only within the last forty-eight hours. It is astonishing how, on Lough Derg, so many are anxious to share their joys and sorrows and quite intimate details of their lives. Then it is time to embark on the boat. The Prior says goodbye to each individual pilgrim and then adds a few parting words for the group. The boat pulls out from the quay and everyone joins in the singing of *Hail Glorious St Patrick*. This is a very emotive moment indeed and I think it makes an indelible mark on each and every pilgrim. I am convinced it is the moment when the desire to return to Lough Derg is born in the human heart.

Eamonn Conway

Finding God on Lough Derg

Generations have trod, have trod, have trod;
And all is seared with trade; bleared, smeared with toil;
And wears man's smudge and shares man's smell: the soil
Is bare now, nor can foot feel, being shod.
Gerard Manley Hopkins

I grew up in Lough Derg. I first came there as a fourth year student for the priesthood in the mid 1980s when Gerard McSorley was Prior. As cantor, I was to look after the singing. It was my first real summer job, also the first time I had to work as part of a team. I had never done the pilgrimage. I remember the first sight of ugly, blistered feet. My reaction: 'How could people be mad enough to do this? They have God all wrong. God does not require this of them. Such a God would be unworthy of worship.'

Then came the litany of the pilgrims: 'How often have you done it?' I knew I had to do the pilgrimage myself. I borrowed rosary beads and began. I settled in quite quickly to the rhythm and the pace of the stations. In some ways it was even easier, certainly more peaceful, than working. I enjoyed the sense of shared journey. I was 'one of them' for a change and they accepted me, simply because I had taken my shoes off. I also enjoyed the challenge. What I missed most was the morning elevenses. After the morning confessions the staff always head down for a cup of tea and Peggy's finest freshly baked scones with homemade jam and butter. The thought of my colleagues enjoying these while I traipsed around the beds more than doubled the penance.

As the pilgrimage continued, I began to understand Lough Derg. This was not about appeasing God, even though some of the more primitive prayers certainly conveyed that impression. This was more about appraising myself. It was about listening to myself bodily and spiritually. It was about getting as much in touch with myself as possible so that I could drag the whole of myself before God. And allow God to shod me, feed me and refresh every fibre of my being. And dragging it was, especially during the vigil night. Those infernal inside stations. Scrambling for the piece of carpet at the altar rails as soon as the word 'kneel' passed the lips of the person leading the station. I remember that I was not asked to lead a station that first time I did the pilgrimage. There was to be no cheap grace for me.

I felt particularly vulnerable going to confession. While other pilgrims were looking for an island priest into whose ears they could tell their sins, confident that their wrongdoings would be left behind them on the island, I was looking for a pilgrim priest who could carry mine off. I remember I found a particularly sympathetic one who was oddly positioned in a corner near the back door of the basilica. I don't remember much of what either of us said. I do remember the sense of healing and reassurance. I also knew that by their prayers, their sacrifice and their humility, others on the island were carrying me.

The rest of the pilgrimage passed quickly and I recall the kindness of fellow staff who provided me with fizzy drinks and my quota of dry toast and Lough Derg oatcakes, and made sure I got straight to bed. It was straight back to work the following day. But I could not wait for a pilgrim to ask me when was the last time I did the pilgrimage.

I got a new insight into the meaning of Lough Derg when I went to Germany as a student in the late 1980s. Occasionally, I used to visit a sports centre and leisure complex near Stuttgart called 'Fildorado'. It had the usual collection of jacuzzis, swimming pools and saunas. It also had an *irisches Dampfbad*, literally an Irish steam bath, a *teach allais* just like those you may still see near the ruins of early Irish monasteries. What fascinated me most, however, was an outside courtyard with small round pebbles. There, people walked around in their bare feet, in circles, following ritual-like patterns. This was supposedly good for their blood circulation.

Fildorado was enough for some people. Others I met in Germany wanted more. They would spend their weekends engaging in the most extreme and dangerous of sports in order to get a 'high': whitewater rafting, skiing off-piste, hang-gliding. Or they would take themselves off to all kinds of religious camps and retreats in the Black Forest in search of the ultimate moment of inner harmony and peace. When I next visited Lough Derg I realised that all my German acquaintances were looking for, and more than many of them ever imagined could be found, was present on a few square yards of bog in a little island in Co Donegal. By God's grace.

I believe that each of us, without exception, deep down craves an experience of unconditional acceptance and love. In an effort to find it sometimes we do strange and silly things. We become addicted, whether to drugs, work or power. We get caught up in unhealthy and destructive relationships. We spend a fortune in therapy or, if we can afford it, on expensive Celtic Tiger toys. We consume the soft-core spiritualities which make even God into a commercial commodity. In the end, none of these satisfy. The lucky ones make their way to a place like Lough Derg.

Lough Derg leaves little room for the luxury of pretence. There, without any of the trappings, the false identities and securities, I meet myself. Meeting myself is traumatic enough. But what can give me the courage to accept myself as I find myself? Only the certain belief that my creator has already done so. In fact, it is only when I recognise that I stand bare, but on the firm ground of God's unshakeable love, that I can have the courage to look at myself as I am, warts and all. Without the knowledge of God's love, the knowledge of my weakness and failure would be too much for me. I could not face it. With the knowledge of God's love, knowledge carved into the stones of this holy island, I can take an honest look at myself. And begin to change.

I began by quoting a few lines from Hopkins' *God's Grandeur*. Hopkins had a keen sense of the presence of God in all things and of the danger that people were becoming desensitised to it: 'nor does the foot feel, being shod'. Lough Derg may be one of the few places left where feet continue to feel, and where, with each painful step taken, God's grandeur and graciousness are unmistakably impressed upon body and spirit. May generations continue to tread and treasure this holy island.

Eileen Byrne

Remembered by an old photograph

My first impression of Lough Derg is summed up on the back of an old photograph I have. It reads:

Lough Derg August 1952
May, myself, M. Connolly
The weather was cruel, the journey long, the fasting awful
The black tea and soup the limit, no sleep – the last word
But it was worth it all.

A native of Kildare, I spent most of my working years in Limerick where about thirty of us came together every year to do the pilgrimage to Lough Derg. We would hire a bus for the journey and make no other plans until 'after Lough Derg'.

On the appointed day of the pilgrimage, we were off at six o'clock in the morning and as everyone knew each other it was greetings all around, like 'How are you Mary? I didn't see you since last year,' or 'Is that yourself Tom? It's younger you're getting', and so on as we journeyed to our destination. It was more like a festive occasion than a pilgrimage, until we reached the island. This was the pattern every time down through the years but, sorry to say, a new face now and again replaced a regular pilgrim as they were called to their eternal reward. A bereavement always caused sadness to us all.

At last we were on the island and if the weather was fine it was a great consolation, for come rain, hail or sunshine, the stations had to be done, the fasting and vigil to follow. Everyone has a purpose in going to Lough Derg, the sick, the bereaved, students, business people and people of every walk of life; you will meet them all and if you want to see dedication go there yourself. You would be amazed to see hundreds of people bare-footed praying and fasting on one meal a day of dry toast and black tea.

It's great when the exercises are over and you listen to all the yarns about getting there, going astray on the journey and, above all, not knowing what to expect on your first visit. A relation of mine thought she was going to Lough Derg on the Shannon and packed her swim gear; and there was the time we decided to go by car after work. We started off at 6.00 pm to stay in Sligo for the night and have a meal. I think we did half of Ireland before we got there. The meal extended beyond midnight. I told the Prior the next day. Guess what? He told us to fast by winter, or old time!

Then there was the time of the postal strike. We didn't know when Lough Derg opened. I asked the Bishop of Limerick could he find out for us. He said he would do his best. He contacted St Macartan's College in Monaghan and made arrangements that they would contact us, which they did. Fr Joseph Duffy, who had been a member of staff at Lough Derg, rang us. He told me he had good news and bad news. The good news was, he wouldn't be going back to Lough Derg that year – 1979. I asked him why. He said, 'I can't tell you that but you'll know soon'. About a week later I opened the paper and there was Bishop Duffy's photo saying he was the youngest bishop in Ireland. I never got a chance to say congratulations until last year and do you know what he said? 'Are you still around?' It was a great laugh.

Another time, we were crossing over in the boat – a good many years ago now – and it was a cold and rainy day as usual and we were saying wasn't it a pity we couldn't wear slacks and these four or five women said, 'Oh but you can wear slacks now. We have permission.' And, raising the hem of their skirts, they were all in slacks! Were we jealous, because we hadn't got the message as yet. It was great news because the following year slacks were the height of fashion because of their suitability and comfort.

As I'm retired now and have been to Lough Derg about seventy times, I often contemplate on things that impress me most; like the stillness of the night, of the vigil, three or four hundred walking around the basilica in silent prayer, the lapping of the lake, the coolness of the ground and everything that makes life uncomfortable, especially lack of sleep. Many, many people from the North go to Lough Derg praying for peace. One man I often met there was the late Eddie McAteer MP whose plea was always for peace in the North. I'm sure God has answered his Lough Derg prayer.

Many changes have been made down through the years. We no longer get the smell of the turf fires as we approach the shore. That smell always reminded me of days gone by. Toilet facilities and dormitories have been upgraded, but one thing that never changes is the rigour of the pilgrimage exercises. They never have and I hope they never will. The final thought of my most recent pilgrimage was on that little bird who built her nest right beside St Brigid's Bed hoping to rear five little ones. What a brave creature.

As I always say leaving the island, 'God willing, I'll come back next year.'

James Byers

A moment of eternity

I first went to Lough Derg in 1995, when I was fifteen. My family had already been several times and I had heard many graphic stories from my sisters. Mum, however, maintained that it was not that difficult for your first time. Young and impressionable, I listened. After all, she had done the pilgrimage more than twenty times. Her mission now was to introduce each of her four off-spring to St Patrick's Purgatory.

Belfast to Pettigo was a long and apprehensive journey, especially when your stomach is not just rumbling but growling at this stage! On leaving Pettigo, only one tiny winding road led to Lough Derg. My sisters, groaning ever louder as we viewed the dark misty waters to our right, announced: 'This is it.' I looked over the lake where some grey dismal, prison-like buildings sprouted from the horizon. There was no going back.

I completed the first three stations without too much affliction, and having feasted on a Lough Derg meal, I felt relatively elated.

Then the long rigorous night loomed ahead. At six thirty Mass that evening, I remember being really in awe of the fine music and singing. I readily joined in and it was at that time that I vowed to join my parish Folk Group with my trusty flute.

At the beginning of 1997 I wrote to the Prior, Mgr Mohan, asking to be considered for a summer job and was subsequently offered the position of cantor. My first day was very nerve wracking, but I was helped and supported by the very experienced organist Louise Kelly.

My position as cantor was not only to lead and encourage some hearty singing, but also to talk and listen to the pilgrims as they carried out their pilgrimage. One aspect I did not anticipate was the 6.00 am starts to prepare the sanctuary for early morning Mass. However, I must admit, I actually came to enjoy the fresh early mornings as I walked from my dormitory to the basilica, looking at the sky and trying to forecast the weather.

The pilgrimage is demanding, no doubt about it. So what are those *je ne sais quoi* qualities which bring you back again and again? I suppose each person is drawn in their own special way, but for me it is the personal, spiritual space and of course the music. This is something which I can contribute to which brings its own kind of reward for me. The opportunity to look inwards at your whole self, and find out where you are in relation to your God, is not easy in the busy coming and goings of life but, having left all material trappings on the mainland, on Lough Derg you have no other choice.

Lough Derg has something to offer everyone, old and young; all individuals on an equal footing. Some may think it is outdated, medieval, but experience it at least once and, like so many of our Irish ancestors, you will know spiritual well-being and a new awareness of yourself as a person. At the beginning of the twenty-first century, we can scarcely imagine the world of twenty years from now, but the Lough Derg pilgrims are happy to continue with the traditions of thousands of years, to be barefooted, to be fasting, to maintain the twenty-four hour vigil and to be a simple human being like all other pilgrims around you on a little island in a moment of eternity.

Mary Briody

St Patrick's Purgatory – Heaven or Hell?

I'm not sure whether events look better or worse with the passage of time. Now that I'm safely away from Lough Derg where one has to fast, pray and be deprived of sleep and shoes, I think I can venture to write a piece on the experience there. I write both from the viewpoint of a pilgrim and as a member of staff.

Firstly, as a pilgrim I was one of those poor creatures going around with a hungry and tired look on their faces. One of those who would hover at the lake's edge in the hope that a juicy fish would jump up into their arms. Were you one of those pilgrims or were you one of those who attempted to bribe some of the staff into smuggling some food over from the staff building where the lovely home cooking smells came from? Some pilgrims claimed they could smell an Ulster Fry in the mornings coming from that self-same building, but I reckon they were hallucinating and imagining all sorts of things after their sleep-deprived night.

I have only done the pilgrimage twice in all but hope to attempt it again in the future. I have to say it is one of the hardest pilgrimages going. For me, I think the lack of sleep during the vigil is the toughest part – the temptation to nod off to sleep is nearly overpowering. I remember the first time I did the pilgrimage; I found the night part of the vigil fine. I stayed awake no problem at all and even got a giggle or two from observing those sleepy heads around me – including my father and brother. Peoples' heads bobbing up and down and the dazed look on their faces when they wakened was hilarious – it kept me amused all night. Who needs television when you have all this around you?

However, the next day everything wasn't quite as amusing.

Tiredness hit me like a sack of spuds being dropped on one's toes – ouch! I was flicking through a book in the bookshop when it came over me. One minute I was saying to myself 'This looks like an interesting book', the next, I was waking with a jump. Anyway this was just the mild part of the day, the worst was yet to come. Due to the lack of sleep I was like a bear with a sore head. I had taken on the persona of the 'Incredible Hulk', not green but very angry! So at this stage it was God help anyone who trod on my toes. So I decided that the best mode of action was to steer clear of all human beings.

Just as Jesus withdrew for forty days in the desert, I too withdrew to the water's edge to face my own demons. At this point the anger had gone and sadness came to fill its place. I was in bits for a few hours and needed that time to myself to regain my composure to face the world again.

Time spent on Lough Derg is invaluable; one has time to take stock of one's life – to see where one is at and where one is going. It's 'timeout' from the hustle and bustle. People's 'airs and graces' are cast aside with their shoes and everyone is on the one level – barefooted! Being on Lough Derg brings a clarity to one's life – you see what's important and what's not.

The other side of the Lough Derg coin was being there as a member of staff. I have to say that this was a more enjoyable time spent on Lough Derg. In contrast to the pilgrimage stay, where one usually loses weight, if one is working there one gains weight due to the brilliant home-cooked food. The lovely home-made lemon meringue pie and ice cream stick out in my mind. The food was a popular topic of conversation with the pilgrims; some pilgrims actually thought that the staff got the same as them, namely dry toast and black tea or coffee. I filled them in on what we really got to eat – I don't know why water suddenly gushed out from the sides of their mouths, it must have been something I said!

I worked on Lough Derg in the summer of 1999 for nearly six weeks as a member of the pastoral team along with another young fellow who was training to be a priest. The two of us held discussion groups in the afternoons and helped out around the basilica. It was a privileged position to be working in, out among the pilgrims serving God. Some of the discussion groups got quite heated (debate-wise) which meant that nobody nodded off to sleep. Other times there were issues raised that brought a tear to the eyes of a pilgrim or two and it wasn't the leaking roof!

I am certain that in my time working there I felt closer to God than I normally would in my everyday life. I actually felt a peace, happiness and contentment in myself that I don't experience too often. There is definitely something spiritual and special about that little island on Lough Derg in remote, wild Donegal which should be held onto for future generations.

Michael Breslin

Never again – but we do, don't we?

I don't remember much about my early Lough Derg pilgrim-ages, except I could never understand people laughing and jok-ing through the open door where a fire was blazing merrily, right beside the large penitential bed.

Less so in later years, when as an adult now I was making a conscious effort to focus. By then I was able to synchronise my four times around the basilica with the requisite seven decades. Speed was still a bit of a problem and I chaffed at the awkward-ness of those in front of me negotiating the stony traps of St Brigid's Bed and the way they clung for dear life to the cross in the centre.

But, I got over that too. There weren't as many old people as in earlier years – the One-Day Retreats had seen to that, but there were still one or two. I came to admire their sense of quiet devotion and all those misshapen toes.

At the end of last year's pilgrimage, the Monsignor, as usual, came on board the boat to wish us well and he suggested we might come back next year. Some wag shouted they would if they could have butter on the toast and milk in the tea. 'And we'll tarmac St Brigid's Bed as well,' he retorted. We all laughed at that yet I know for certain no one wanted anything to change.

I don't know who coined the phrase 'a tough station', but it surely fits St Patrick's Purgatory. For me, the fasting, the dry toast and black tea and the beds aren't the worst. It's the Vigil that's the killer, especially that moment when those departing the next morning head for bed.

Four stations of repetitive prayer, each lasting an hour – is there a Commando course anywhere that is equal to it? I doubt it. But, thinking on it is no solution. What I found myself doing was becoming immersed in the multiplicity of repeated patterns people employed.

There were those who like myself went round and round, others slapped back and forth outside the door, others went to and fro' along the same row of seats and still others did the same parallels with the altar rails.

Then one year I was asked to give out a Station. I readily agreed as I think everyone does. One nice thing about the vigil is that it is people-driven, no priest in sight, save those doing the pilgrimage. I suppose I was petrified at the very start. I was now the conductor of a disparate orchestra but, once started, I felt a power. Here I was dictating their very movements for the next hour. I was sensitive to their unspoken needs and finished in less than the hour. It's amazing how people can measure time on such an occasion. 'Well done, you kept it galloping along,' was one reaction as I drew with relief on my Silk Cut in the old hostel at the break.

The Station after that was a real breeze. You gave a wink of encouragement to the next giver-out every time you passed and, in between, measured their performance. You noticed they were taking short cuts, dropping an Our Father along the way until a nun went up and corrected them.

It takes the nuns. They don't miss a trick.

The second day has to be the most relaxing day one can get anywhere in the world. You've done night patrol and survived its worst excesses, including lack of sleep of course. And that Sacrament of Reconciliation, well it beats the old-style Confession any day. How our young minds ever got over the trauma of being enclosed in darkness and telling your sins through a grille to someone whose face you never saw full frontal, I'll never know. I don't think Jesus Christ would have approved. Rather, he would have touched you gently on the arm or shoulder and spoken words of comfort.

What he would have thought of Lough Derg, I don't know. But, if fasting and penance – which he did himself for forty days we're told – is the gateway to heaven, then I'd like to think that's where I'm heading.

But I'll go this year anyhow and after that, well, we'll see.

Greg Blaney

A father remembered

When I hear of or think about Lough Derg I immediately think of my father, Sean Blaney, who died there on 11 July 1996 from a heart attack. Despite the great feeling of loss associated with his death I think it was a good way to die and a good place to spend the last few days of his life on this earth. He was a great believer in the value of prayer and the one piece of advice that he always gave to myself and the rest of my family was 'keep saying your prayers'.

The other things which I associate with Lough Derg are lack of sleep and food, although these negative thoughts are quickly followed by remembering how good I always feel on completing the pilgrimage. As well as being a place of prayer and penance, Lough Derg is also a great place for meeting people of all ages and backgrounds. There always seems to be a great sense of togetherness on the island, everyone realising that no-one finds it easy. The removal of all footwear on beginning the pilgrimage is, for me, very symbolic. The pilgrims may come from all walks of life but in the eyes of God we are all equal.

Whenever I am finding the going tough I look around at the number of older people doing the pilgrimage and I think that it shouldn't be too hard for me. Their ability to endure the stones, the fasting and the weather is an inspiration to the younger generation.

I find that for me, as well as the prayer and the penance, Lough Derg is a good place to take stock and also to take a break from the hustle and bustle of everyday life. It certainly is a weekend break with a difference! Each year I go to Lough Derg I don't find it any easier but I keep going back. I have a fairly pampered lifestyle 362 days of the year so I reckon a few days in Lough Derg does me no harm. However, I know that no matter how often I go there, and throughout the time I spend there, my thoughts will always return to my father.

Terri Ball

'And the flesh became word'

In recent years I have spent time on Lough Derg, not as a pilgrim but as counsellor, a listener, encouraging those who want to speak, to risk it, yes, risk it.

Some come to me to speak, saying that they will only be five minutes. They have a prepared five-minute script. An hour later they finish, though they could go on. Delivering a script is not speaking, just as acting a part – what we do most of the time – is not living, but the speaking starts when the script is discarded and one dares to allow the flesh to become word – just as one dares on Lough Derg, to allow the flesh to become sore – to become word in its own way and to live, even momentarily, outside the safe confines of a scripted reality.

To speak in this way is to be a part of the ongoing work of creation. To speak in this way is also to be part of the ongoing mystery of incarnation because that which is truly spoken shatters the familiar script within which we have learned to act, thus creating the crack through which new light is thrown on truth, the truth of who we are and the truth of who God is.

The crack, just like a crack of dawn on Lough Derg, is both welcome and unwelcome; welcome because the light indicates the beginning of the end of a painful night, and unwelcome because the day is long and the flesh is sore. But it is the crack, the dawn, the dawning that allows one to hope.

The difference between living an unscripted life, as opposed to living the scripted life of playing the role one has been given by others, is like the difference between taking part in a scripted play and taking part in improvised drama. In the former there are first the rehearsals, then comes the actual production. In the latter, every rehearsal is a final production just as every production is a rehearsal – risky, yes, but forever new and open to possibilities and surprises.

What is the incarnation if it is not a statement of the reality that this life is not a dress-rehearsal? And yet, how often we live life as though we were practising a script in the hope of getting it right when the time comes! And what is creation if not a statement of the reality that, for the Word to become flesh in incarnation, the flesh must become word in creation. Furthermore, it is only when the flesh becomes sore that the flesh then seeks to become word in the speaking.

When flesh becomes sore then flesh becomes word,
And the work of creation goes on
And the Word becomes flesh ... again.

Anonymous

Lough Derg, the great leveller

The narrow twisty road out from Pettigo, the small, poor fields on each side. The uneasy feeling in the pit of your stomach. Around the last bend and there it is, the basilica sitting in the middle of the lake. 'Oh my God, what am I doing here again?'

The first time I went to Lough Derg, with my father and brother, we were transported to the island with forty or fifty others in a big rowing boat about thirty foot long, with three enormous oars or sweeps on each side and two local men on each sweep. When the blade dipped in the water the man on the inside of the sweep had to jump up on the bench to pull; local men, strong and ruddy faced. My brother and I called them 'the skins'. God knows what they called us!

Lough Derg, the great leveller. When you went on the island you weren't a captain of industry or a bishop or a worker. When you took off your shoes, tried not to wince on the sharp stones, tried not to fall asleep at night, tried not to feel too hungry, you were no better nor no worse than the person beside you. Worldly distractions became irrelevant and you were ready to talk to God and hope he might listen.

Nor did your 'religion' matter. Catholic, Protestant, Buddhist, whatever, the island handled them all. Some liked it, some did not. I remember an American parish priest standing outside the basilica at 6.00 o'clock one morning, grey-faced after the vigil, facing the lake. Without warning he said, 'God damn it – what am I doing here?' I saw him leaving on the first boat out that morning.

My own wife, an active Church of Ireland member, came with me to Lough Derg many a time. She was always quick on the last station before leaving. We were warned not to hurry this last station, but there was always a little group out in front, trying to look humble and holy but at the same time anxious not to be passed out! One stocky, tough Belfast man sitting beside me washing his feet remarked, 'that wee wife of yours is pretty quick around the beds'. 'Yes,' I replied, adding, 'You know she is a Protestant?' 'My God,' he said, 'You mean to tell me I have to go back to Belfast and tell them I was beaten on Lough Derg by a Prod?'

Why does one go to Lough Derg? God only knows. But I do know that it is one of the very special places in Ireland and probably in the world. May it survive another thousand years.

Anonymous

A Munster pilgrimage to an Ulster Shrine
(Written circa 1898)

In my childhood I may have heard of Lough Derg but like most southerners I had only a very vague and perhaps mixed idea of the holy lake and its associations. I say mixed, because of the Tyrconnell pilgrimage being frequently confounded with the other Lough Derg, the expansion of the Shannon. However, the recent writings in the *Messenger of the Sacred Heart* and an interesting little article in the Christmas number of the *Loreto Magazine* cleared away all erroneous opinions I had acquired about Lough Derg and filled me with a strong desire to visit this time-honoured sanctuary amid the Donegal mountains.

The difficulties of transit, the distance of the place and fear of expense often deter us southerners from such a venture. However, I was determined to go and wrote to a friend in Dublin to make inquiries from some of the priests in the diocese of Clogher which would facilitate my journey, with the result that I availed of an excursion to Dublin in July which lasted a week to make my visit to the 'island'. Had I gone alone from Dublin, the excursion ticket, third class return, would have cost me nearly £1, but having the good fortune to be permitted to join a party of seven, the return ticket was less than 10s. We started from Dublin by the 2.45 pm train, one of our party pointing out places of interest along the way. The scenes which impressed me most were the town of Drogheda, viewed below us as we crossed the Boyne viaduct, and the glorious lake and mountain scenery along Lough Erne, glimpses of which we caught from time to time out of the train while looking southwards. Arrived at Pettigo about half-past seven, we got out of the train and some of our party who had been there before ordered cars for us. Several other people came by the same train; some stopped in the village but the majority, like ourselves, insisted on cars being brought out and drove direct to the lake which we reached shortly after eight, after passing through agricultural and into mountainous country.

The first view of the lake was rather disappointing, but as we passed round the side of the mountain the scene much improved until we ultimately got a view of the peculiar little island called Station Island, which we looked at with much interest until we saw a boat rowed towards us from the island. When the boat arrived we gave the car proprietor 9d and the boatman 8d each which paid for our transit to and from the island. A dozen of us were rowed over by exceedingly careful boatmen, and on landing on the island quay I was greatly inclined to stand and stare about me at the number of men and women walking about bareheaded and barefooted; but the lady who piloted our party from the start hurried me away to the ladies' hospice where I was allotted a little one-windowed cell furnished with a bed, dressing-table, and one chair.

Soon after our arrival a bell announced the Stations of the Cross. We went out to St Patrick's Church where the congregation consisted of about two hundred of men and women, ladies and gentlemen of all ages and positions, every one bareheaded and barefooted except those of us who had just arrived; and it was most peculiar to see them all move silently round the Stations of the Cross, led by a priest and acolyte. When the devotion had concluded, we returned to the hospice, where we sat down to a light supper. I must admit that my heart would have failed me, had not those of my friends who had been there before cheered me on during the meal, after which we retired to bed. A sound sleep was broken in on by the tolling of a bell at half-past four, summoning all those on the island to arise and dress in time for five o'clock Mass and, like every one else in the hospice, I walked out barefooted for the first time in my life. All my friends chatted and jested about the straits we were reduced to.

We entered the church, heard five o'clock Mass, which concluded with an interesting discourse from the celebrant, a young priest. On leaving the church after Mass, I contemplated my surroundings. The island on which we were is a mile from the end of the great lake, dotted with other islands, which extended about six miles in length by four miles in width. All round the lakeshore are mountains or high hills on which very few habitations are visible. Station Island itself is small and one is inclined to wonder how there was room for so many buildings on it. First there is St Patrick's Church which covers the whole northern portion of the island. It is built, like most country churches, without any pretension to architecture. Next to it along the western shore of the island is the hospice, at the southern end of which are some lodging-houses, terminating with the presbytery beside the quay on which we had landed. Opposite the presbytery is St Mary's Church, not so large as St Patrick's but much nearer and more architectural. The space between St Patrick's and St Mary's and facing the hospice, consists of the rocky little hill on the top of which is the campanile; and on the slope facing St Patrick's there are six stone circles with crucifixes in the centre which are called beds. Between these beds and the hospice are three beautiful white marble statues of Our Blessed Lady, St Patrick, and St Joseph. The statues are raised on pedestals about eight feet from the ground. Even in our own city there is hardly a more beautiful statue than that of St Patrick.

At the southern gable of St Patrick's Church there is a stone pillar about four feet high and six inches in diameter, with a little metal cross in the head of it. This pillar is called St Patrick's Cross and is evidently of great antiquity. Like most of our Irish religious relics, it has received bad treatment at the hands of our heretical conquerors. It has been broken across near the base and the crucifix which is now replaced by the little metal cross has been long since destroyed; the very socket of it, along with the capital of the pillar, has been broken. There are some other ancient stones; one appears to be the tomb of St MacNisse who died AD 514.

When our party had concluded our inspection of the island

we entered the church with the intention of beginning our first penitential exercise, called a station, which began by a visit to the Blessed Sacrament in St Patrick's Church. We proceeded thence to St Patrick's Cross where we knelt and recited a Pater, Ave and Credo, at the conclusion of which we proceeded round the back of St Patrick's Church to St Brigid's Cross, which is merely a Maltese cross carved on a slab in the wall of St Patrick's Church. Before this we recited three Paters, three Aves and a Credo kneeling. Each one then stood up, turned his or her back to the cross and silently renounced the world, the flesh, and the devil three times. This was followed by seven circuits of St Patrick's Church. During each circuit one decade of the Rosary was recited; to the decade was added on the last circuit the Credo. We then walked up the hill to the 'beds'. The first bed is dedicated to St Brigid. We made three external circuits of it during which we said three Paters, three Aves and a Credo. We knelt at the entrance of the bed, saying the same prayers which we also repeated while making three internal circuits and while kneeling at the crucifix in the centre of the bed. We then proceeded to the next bed, St Brendan's, where the same prayers and exercises were said and performed. These two beds are very rocky and were the most difficult parts of the station I met with. The next two beds at which the same penitential exercises were performed were much easier. The first, the patron of which is uncertain, is said by some to be dedicated to a St Catherine, and by others to St Dabhog (Davoc), the founder of the ancient monastery which flourished here. There are two more beds dedicated to St Molaise and St Patrick, around which similar exercises were performed. Having finished at the last, we went to the water's edge, where five Paters, five Aves and a Credo were recited standing, and the same while kneeling. Instead of standing at the edge of the water most of us stood in the water. We returned then to whence we started, to St Patrick's Cross where we recited kneeling one Pater, one Ave and a Credo. We then entered St Patrick's Church where we formed a little group in the seats, and we joined in reciting five decades of the Rosary, and five Paters, Aves and Glorias for the Pope's intentions. This brought the station to a close, which lasted nearly an hour and a half. We then went out and had a pleasant chat over the novelty of our experiences. We all felt in high spirits and most of us were quite exuberant. We re-entered the church and made a second station exactly as we had done the first and, after a little rest and some more talk, some of us did a third station. This concluded the entire exercises of the day. I felt rather tired and was recommended to join my friends in taking a cup of 'wine' which consisted of the ironated water of the lake boiled and sweetened with sugar. This had a most rousing effect and acted as quite a tonic; and we chatted and talked over our wine until the noonday Angelus rang.

We then entered St Patrick's Church where a short discourse was delivered by one of the priests suggesting points for meditation. When we left the church I repaired to my cell where I read some chapters of meditation and made a careful preparation for confession which was to take place on the next day. After a couple of hours, one of my friends came to the room and told me it was time to have our meal; and then, for the first time, it struck me I had not eaten anything since the evening before although it was now three o'clock in the afternoon and all the while I did not feel hungry. Around the refectory table fourteen or fifteen of us gathered and sat down to a meagre meal of dry bread and black tea. We laughed and joked over our meal which we really enjoyed. Most of those at the table ate oaten bread while others did not even take the tea but preferred the 'wine'. The afternoon and evening were spent by me in my cell reading and meditating up to 6 pm, when all those on the island assembled in St Patrick's Church for Evening Devotions, Sermon and Benediction. After the Benediction many people who felt strong enough made extra stations for absent and deceased friends. Others of us spent the time pleasantly enough until the Stations of the Cross at nine o'clock in St Patrick's Church; at the conclusion of which we returned to the hospice and refreshed ourselves with more of the 'wine' and entered 'prison' for the night at ten sharp.

The two hours between ten and midnight were spent by us in singing hymns and listening to a man reading meditations. As soon as twelve arrived, a blind man whom I had not previously noticed was led to the altar rails and announced that we were going to do the stations. We all gathered round the altar and said the prayers we had said during the day, standing and kneeling or moving about inside the church to repeat our exercises of the previous day. At the end of the first and second stations we went out into the open air to rouse ourselves but during the third station I felt it very difficult to keep from sleeping. About 4 am we were released from 'prison', and went to the hospice which had been opened by some young girls who wanted to get some stations performed before Mass.

A fire was been lighted in the kitchen and we sat round it and chatted with our new friends until the bell rang at half-past four when I went upstairs and had a wash and came down in time for Mass. All of us who had been doing the vigil the previous night were very hard pressed to keep awake during Morning Prayer, Mass and Sermon; each one kept nudging her neighbour. After Mass some of us made a few extra stations for absent and deceased friends for it is no part of the exercise to make stations on the second day. There was no use in attempting to read, for one was sure to fall asleep.

We went to confession early in St Mary's Church and then refreshed ourselves with 'wine'. There was a pleasure party of which I formed one that went by boat to Saints' Island, the passage over being occupied by singing – the girls singing the hymns and the men singing national songs. On Saints' Island we walked over the broken ground and ruined walls where a great monastery once stood. There is a big stone on it called 'the wishing stone' where, it is said, the wish is granted to those who stand on it and wish aloud in the presence of the fellow-pilgrims. It was very amusing to listen to each person who got on the stone losing courage to express their real desires and generally winding up by wishing for heaven. Some of the young men made patriotic wishes and one lady wished to have a son a priest. A young Donegal girl wished in Irish and was applauded by the men. She got down quite ashamed and in doubt lest some of them understood her. She was far worse when in the boat coming back. We had songs in Irish from two of the men. A pleasant dinner of black tea and dry bread took up an hour of our time, and the rest of the day was spent as best we could – moving about the island, attending the religious exercises and, when awake enough, in reading, seated on the grass in the open air. After the last devotions we bathed our feet and went to bed where I slept soundly until called by a friend in time for Mass when I received Holy Communion. During this third day I made three more stations and fasted as I had done on the previous days. The fourth morning I had great bother in getting on my boots; after which I partook of a hearty breakfast.

We had two hours to spare after breakfast before the boat which runs to catch the train should start and I went with a few friends in the Prior's boat to Port Creevy Bay where we sat in St Brigid's Chair and then ascended Seavog Mountain. On the top there are the remains of a pagan cromlech which St Davoc had used as a cave for solitary retirement. From this place there is a beautiful view of Lough Derg, its mountains and islands; while looking south and west there is a splendid prospect which includes the Cavan, Fermanagh, and Leitrim mountains, with Lough Erne in the foreground to complete the picture. Here I was pointed out the Cuilcagh range where the Shannon rises.

On my return I paid my bill which was only about 5s, gave a small subscription towards the island to the Prior and departed in the boat. I felt quite sad at leaving and could not restrain my tears when a couple of girls commenced singing the *Farewell to Lough Derg*. The car and train brought us quickly from the northern land over the Boyne to Dublin where I spent the night. The next day I returned home, after having spent the happiest week of my life. I liked the northern people greatly and, if their home life is at all in keeping with their life in Lough Derg, they are a very excellent people. When I returned home my friends were astonished at what I had gone through: I who had seldom walked barefooted across my own room, who would not think of going out of doors bareheaded, who had always thought I had mortified myself much with a carefully cooked meal and a good collation on the three black fasts in Lent, who went to bed and slept well every night – had actually done Lough Derg and felt the better of it.

I have heard young men in the south boast of their democracy, I have heard religious ladies and gentlemen express strong opinions on humility, but I can tell all such persons that one visit to Lough Derg will do more to teach them to understand these two than all the speeches and sermons, learned and religious books which they are ever likely to hear or read.

One of the strongest impressions made on me by my pilgrimage was the idea I got of the early Christian Church and how truly the exercises bring one in touch with the times of the early martyrs and saints. The rigid fasts on one meal a day (without even a collation), the severe penance and the isolation of the place, all tend to excite thoughts of those earlier times. Then again the vigil, which in ancient times used to form part of the church's ceremonies during Holy Week and of other festivals, is preserved in Lough Dearg alone of all our northern countries. The traditions, the mysticism and the lively faith which surrounds the holy island make a visit to it the greatest event in the lives of most ordinary people.

Let me appeal to my fellow-citizens, as well as to all Munster people who are patriotically or religiously inclined, who can spare the time and afford the outlay, and who want to spend a really happy week in this world, to make the pilgrimage to St Patrick's Purgatory.

List of Contributors

Anonymous p 11: Scottish pilgrim c1898
Anonymous p 140: Regular Dublin pilgrim.
Anonymous p 144: Female pilgrim from south of Ireland c1898
Ball, Terri: Dublin.
Blaney, Greg: Kircubbin, Co Down. Dentist. All Ireland medalist and GAA Allstar.
Breslin, Michael: Lisnaskea, Co Fermanagh. Journalist.
Briody, Mary: Glenties, Co Donegal. Student teacher.
Byers, James: Newtownards, Co Down. Law student at University of Ulster.
Byrne, Eileen: Castledermott, Co Kildare. Retired secretary.
Cassidy, Anne: Enniskillen, Co Fermanagh. Photographer.
Conway, Eamonn: Priest of Tuam diocese. Head of Department of Theology and Religious Studies University of Limerick.
Corrigan, Paul: Belanaleck, Co Fermanagh. Farmer. Former Chairman of Fermanagh District Council.
Devine, Agnes Mary: Monaghan town. St Louis sister. Retired.
Dowling, Clare: Dublin. Post graduate student at NUI, Maynooth.
Duffy, Pauline: Co Monaghan. Student teacher.
Dyrvik, Stale: Norway. History professor.
Flynn, La: Priest of Clogher Diocese.
Ganni, Ragheed: Iraq. Seminarian in Rome.
Handschin, Judith: Basel, Switzerland. Art Therapist.
Henriot, Vincent: France. Training and Communication manager.
Hogan, Colm: Co Tipperary. Priest of Killaloe Diocese.
Kelly, Louise: Co Monaghan. Primary School Teacher.
Kennedy, Simon: New Ross, Co Wexford. Solicitor.
Lang, Eugen: Basel, Switzerland. Goldsmith.
Leonard, Ann: Co Monaghan. Member of Seanad Eireann.
London Lough Derg Committee. Secretary: Maurice Smyth.
Loughran, Michelle: Co Tyrone. A-level student.
Mallon, Tony: Lurgan, Co Armagh. Industrial Cleaning Contractor.
McAreavey, John: Bishop of Dromore.

McCague, Sean: Scotstown, Co Monaghan. President of Gaelic Athletic
    Association.

McDonagh, James: Coalisland, Co Tyrone. Secondary school student.

McGrath, Fiona: Ballybay, Co Monaghan. V.E.C. Adult Education
    Officer and Director of M.I.F.E.T.

McGregor, Shaun: Draperstown, Co Derry. Teacher, Holy Cross
    College Cookstown, Co Tyrone.

McSorley, Gerard: Parish Priest Ballybay, Co Monaghan. Prior of
    Lough Derg 1980-1990.

Meadon, David: Member of Church of England. Chartered Building
    Surveyor, Chartered Environmental Biologist, Toxicologist.

Olivier, Patricia: France.

Raftery, Peter: C.S.Sp. Teacher, Rockwell College, Cashel, Co
    Tipperary.

Sherrington, John: Priest of Nottingham diocese. Director of Studies at
    St John's Seminary, Wonersh, England.

Snow, Jim: Pettigo, Co Donegal. Former boatman Lough Derg.

Taylor, Alice: Cork. Author.

Thompson, Mary: Irvinestown, Co Fermanagh. Insurance Broker.

Tiernan, Dr Peter: Meath. Retired university lecturer.

Toal, Joe: Priest of Argyle and the Isles. Spiritual Director, Scots
    College, Salamanca, Spain.

Ward, Charlie & Patrick, Coalisland, Co Tyrone. Secondary school
    students.

Wall, Mary: Dublin. P.A. to deputy Chief Executive of Mater hospital.

Walsh, Willie: Bishop of Killaloe.